E QUAKE

A New Approach to Understanding
the End Time Mysteries
in the Book of Revelation

JACK HAYFORD

THOMAS NELSON PUBLISHERS®
Nashville

Published in Nashville, Tennessee, by Thomas Nelson, Inc.

Unless otherwise noted Scripture quotations are from THE NEW KING JAMES VERSION. Copyright © 1979, 1980, 1982, Thomas Nelson, Inc., Publishers.

Scripture quotations noted *The Message* are from *The Message: The New Testament in Contemporary English*. Copyright © 1993 by Eugene H. Peterson.

Library of Congress Cataloging–in–Publication Data

Hayford, Jack W.
    E quake : a new approach to understanding the end time mysteries in the book of Revelation / Jack Hayford.
      p. cm.
    ISBN 0-7852-7472-3 (pbk.)
    1. Bible. N.T. Revelation—Criticism, interpretation, etc.
I. Title.
BS2825.2.H38 1999
228'.06—dc21

                  99–15325
                  CIP

Printed in the United States of America.
3 4 5 6 7 8 QPV 04 03 02 01 00 99

CONTENTS

Contents

INTRODUCTION:
REVELATIONS OF MY OWN

As you open this small book of mine, let me disclose three things.

First, I never planned and didn't want to write a book on the book of Revelation. Then, I *had* to. I didn't want to because I was certain I would be criticized for refusing to take the usual "party line" on the subject of Bible prophecy—I mean, the "line" of pretended *knowingness,* as though traditional charts and interpretations are the "last word" on this last book of the Bible. They aren't, of course. But that doesn't mean I am not certain to disappoint people who find I've taken a different approach. Naturally, I'm not sorry for what I'm offering here, but I didn't want to labor with inevitable criticism . . . until.

Until, second, I was urged over and over, "Pastor Jack, this has to be put on paper for people who want something practical and livable out of Revelation's pages." Of course! Don't we all?! And frankly, I don't think Jesus ever intended His Revelation to the Church to be otherwise. I can't imagine Him giving us something for the mere cultivation or speculation or nurturing of sensationalized interpretations. Accordingly, I sought and found a *nourishing, works-in-your-life* approach, and I've tried to put it here clearly. But there's one more thing—a third "revelation" I must disclose.

The publisher wouldn't let me write it "my way."

Let me be clear, I'm not complaining, but you deserve to know this because it drastically affects the form in which you are receiving this book. My friend at Thomas Nelson Publishers, Victor Oliver, who has been such a great help and encouragement in this project, said, "Jack, I don't want you to write this like you do most of your books. They are fine, but you tend to write to a different audience from the one you preach to every week. By the time you finish editing your books, they may be excellent but they are too academic. I want you to let us publish *E Quake* right from the transcripts of your Sunday sermons!" He insisted on this.

So here you are. With very limited editing and far less exactitude than I would prefer, I am submitting this book with a "revelation" of a residual fear: I'm afraid I'm about to discover people will like this simpler form more than my more labored efforts—an awkward discovery when you're into your thirty-fifth book!

In any case, please know my gratitude for being able to present this to you in any form whatsoever. I trust this approach, in style as well as content, will be as refreshing as it was in the fall of 1998 when God touched multitudes, in my flock as well as over the media, as I presented these less than perfect studies. (If they seem too colloquial at points, you might revert to one of my earlier tomes!)

Should you desire deeper development of the themes opened up here, I have done far more elaborate chapter-by-chapter coverages at other times. Our audiocassette ministry at Living Way (818-779-8000) can service you with those, as well as accompanying study outlines, if you wish.

May our Resurrected, Reigning, and Soon-Coming Savior enrich your heart and life as you and I traverse these pages together.

Sincerely, in Jesus' name,

Jack Hayford
Pastor, The Church on the Way
President, The King's Seminary
14300 Sherman Way
Van Nuys, California 91405

1

THE
BIG
ONE

It was 4:30 A.M. as I slipped back under the covers. I turned over to note that just as I had returned from the bathroom, Anna had risen to make an early-morning visit. I plumped my pillow in the darkness—a tiny night-light providing the only glimmer in the room—then came the explosion.

Indescribable fury! A cataclysmic roar!

Sounds of shattering glass crashing everywhere in the house. Furniture toppling in the room and the sounds of destruction thundering through the whole house.

Horrendous helplessness!

Without there having been the slightest rumble of warning in advance, the room was instantly and powerfully being shaken with a violence that threw me across the bed, forcing me to spin sideways, pushing my body against the headboard. I had no capacity for movement against the seismic forces being unleashed!

Unable to move toward the bathroom where my wife was, I tried to call to her—screaming her name above the grinding shriek of subterranean tides of rock at war with one another. *"ANNA! ANNA!"* I didn't know it, but she had been smashed facedown by an irresistible hand as she had started back to bed, and she was also screaming *my* name. Neither of us could hear the other above the roar, even though we were only fifteen feet apart.

Time seemed suspended. As the incredibly violent shaking continued, I cried out a prayer, "Father, sustain us, please! Sustain us by Your strong hand." My mind inquired, *Is this the End?* It was no melodramatic thought: anyone who had experienced other southern California earthquakes knew the difference. This was in a category *apart!*

The initial shock was less than one minute long, but that seemingly eternal instant emanated shock waves from twelve miles below the floor of the San Fernando Valley in Los Angeles, tearing buildings as if they were paper, splitting freeways as if they were toys, and it became *the most expensive natural disaster in American history.* Further, the $50 billion expended in the aftermath of the upheaval was nothing in comparison to the agonizing pain in the loss of human life, the thousands injured amid falling debris, flying furniture, and shards of glass.

From Fillmore on the north (fifty miles from downtown) to Anaheim on the south (where the big "A" at Angels' Stadium crashed to the ground nearly fifty miles from the epicenter), the earth shook, split, and thundered. The Los Angeles Coliseum was riddled and rubbled, requiring $33 million in repairs before the fall football season that year.

It was January 17, 1994—4:31 A.M.—the day of the Northridge earthquake.

BEEN THERE—DONE THAT

It wasn't as if it was my first ride on a tectonic roller coaster. In February 1971—less than two years after our family had moved to the San Fernando Valley—a 6.4 magnitude quake had broken the morning stillness at six o'clock. I got the worst floor burns since my college basketball days as I tried to crawl down the hall to our children's bedroom while the house shook back and forth beneath me as though giant hands were shaking me like dice and about to throw me into the air. More than sixty people were killed in that quake, including scores dead when a hospital in Sylmar collapsed—a six-story-high wall simply disappearing.

Any effort at describing the viciousness, horror, and violence of 1994's event is not born of its being a once-and-only experience and thereby subject to the exaggeration of a novice. I'd "been there—done that." I was born in Los Angeles, I was raised in the earthquake-prone San Francisco–Oakland Bay area, and for nearly the whole forty years of my pastoral ministry I have lived in southern California. With my family, we've navigated the unsettled terrain of the southland through any number of significant seismic explosions, but nothing has come close to the event of January 17.

For the first weeks following the Northridge quake, seismologists had their own kind of roller-coaster ride, attempting to assess exactly what happened. Years later, the bottom line is that they still don't completely know. It isn't a matter of their being untrained or unintelligent people. Those who try to deduce conclusive answers when nature blows up in their faces simply don't have the resources. With humanly limited technological capabilities and short-term historical data and details, those pursuing so young a field of science as seismology are at an enormous disadvantage when required to explain *why* to all of us.

Their first reports suggested the possibility of *two* earthquakes—a very brief but very violent shock on a fault running from Fillmore to Valencia, then triggering the explosive potential of a second fault, one previously unknown under Northridge, near the center of the San Fernando Valley and its nearly two million inhabitants. Those three communities form something of a lopsided triangle with sides approximately eight to twenty miles long. With the inconsistency of the degree of severity in damage made there and elsewhere, the efforts at explanation became all the more mystifying.

The reality of the scientists' inability to clearly define this quake is evidenced in the fact that the 6.8 magnitude first assigned to the quake seemed so inadequate to explain the scope and degree of destruction. A three-story apartment house pancaked, killing fifteen; shredded parking structures and demolished freeways looked like a European city after a massive bombing raid in World War II; more than one hundred thousand buildings were destroyed or damaged, with multitudes evacuated as their dwellings were declared unsafe for habitation.

At least one seismographic report indicated a 7.2 magnitude, as scientists attempted to explain that the variances in reporting were due to the unusual *vertical* motion of the quake—up and down instead of the more common side-to-side action of temblors. Another report, though unverified publicly, indicated estimates of what the *actual* measurements would have been region by region if the Richter scale were designed to measure vertical motion with the same accuracy it does horizontal action. This report projected the likelihood that the *actual* force of the quake was a staggering 9.6 at its center, reading out at an 8.3 force where Anna and I live in the Granada Hills area. On a scale of 10, it's easy to see why many of us living in Los Angeles had apparent reason to wonder that morning, *Is this the End Quake—the earthquake that will end global history?*

THE E QUAKE

The term *the Big One* is as common to a Californian's vocabulary as *surfboard, Dodger Stadium,* or the *Stars' Walk of Fame* on Hollywood Boulevard. It refers to an oft-alluded to and dubiously anticipated earth rupture forthcoming in our area. There isn't a news watcher or a moviegoer in the world who hasn't heard of the San Andreas Fault—the 500-mile-long scar that creases the state from the San Francisco area southward. Doomsday predictions have been announced at every level—from cultish "kooks" to studied scientists to charismatic prophets to serious analysts of biblical prophecy.

Most commonly, seismologists suggest an impending *7 point plus* quake is imminent, one that is said will be devastating beyond imagination in comparison to the San Fernando Valley's Northridge disaster—an event of profoundly drastic proportions. The most severe possibilities suggested are by those who propose a scenario something like the one depicted in the 1980s

Superman movie with Christopher Reeve. Though the film's story line is ludicrous, the seismic potentiality it centers on is real. There is an arguably real possibility of a mammoth cataclysm ripping California in half; either sinking the westernmost land mass or submerging only the Los Angeles area, then leaving the rest as an uninhabited island. The picture is painted with the deaths of multiple millions—all inhabitants having been washed to sea in the tidal wave accompanying the quake. That is the worst-case scenario whenever *the Big One* is mentioned.

But a prophecy in the Bible proclaims the certainty of a worldwide earthquake that would make our Northridge quake seem hardly more jarring than a supermarket parking lot's speed bump and rank California's projected split-off into the Pacific more comparable to a splash in the backyard pool. The book of Revelation tells of the *End Quake—the E Quake* that ignited the question in my mind that morning, amid the roiling, rolling, rumbling moments Anna and I experienced along with millions of other Californians on that dark, dark day when I asked, *Is this the End?*

Such a question is not born of mere superstition or a religious idea run wild. Instead, it's framed by the findings of contemporary science—by scholars who prophesy the absolute certainty that our planet has an inescapable appointment with a colossal, globe-encompassing earthquake. Still, the Bible's book of Revelation does contain this prophecy—*indeed, it is to a large degree built around it!* It was more than nineteen hundred years ago, and while its message may go unheeded—seeming irrelevant or too mystical to some who prefer to remain unthinking—

I'd like to encourage a more investigative, more thoughtful course of pursuit.

Since the Revelation is so clear about the fact and implications of so unthinkable an event as the virtual disintegration of life as we know it on our planet, and since the most coolheaded scientists are agreed that the inevitable fulfillment of that prophecy could be imminent (and, most believe, unavoidable), perhaps we might give more serious attention to the book.

The book of Revelation is the newspaper of tomorrow, but it is also a handbook for today. It forecasts a series of terrible and terrifying events, but at the same time it provides a perspective on the whole that affords us very practical hope. As a pastor who has sought to nurture my people with the practical instead of the theoretical, and the substantial instead of the speculative, I avoided the Revelation for far too long. My aversion was not related to my perception of the book itself, but was created by the aura of superficial excitement or the almost cultish mysticism I encountered in people almost anytime it was mentioned.

I was also disturbed by the practice of the many interpreters of the Bible who cast almost all of the book's events into a future that they said most readers would never experience or into a past that they said was "prophecy already fulfilled" and only recorded in Revelation symbolically as a historical lesson. Not only were these approaches intellectually unsatisfying by reason of forced interpretations I saw as mandated by the writers' unjustified presuppositions, but they didn't align with the obvious context of the book.

More for the "Now" Than the "Then"

The Revelation *does* deal with the future. It is the consummate "end of times" statement in the Bible! Its Greek name—*The Apocalypse*—provides us with one of the most common words in the English language to be used in describing the awfulness and horror of mankind's worst prospects or most self-destructive machinations. There *are* prophecies in Revelation that will not be fulfilled in the natural lifetime of anyone living now— *true!* But even *more truly* to the facts of the whole book is the dominant objective of the Giver of the book to the writer.

The book of Revelation is given to each of us for our *now— our todays*. First and foremost, it was given by Jesus to speak into the lives of His own, His disciples who, like John, to whom He gave the book for transmission to us, are facing tough realities in an often-hostile setting. It is a gift of comfort for "this day," accompanied by a message of assurance for each "next day." The "last days" issues in Revelation are not incorporated for the purpose of inviting our guessing games about the symbols used or the events they prefigure. Instead, Jesus discloses the future as a paradigm of the present, saying, "As certainly as My Father's purposes will realize His ultimate triumph, so certainly can that same victory invade your present struggle!"

A Book for Everyday People

The Northridge earthquake was experienced by millions—and it sent all of us into days of struggle, some with pain and the deaths of dear ones, some with the loss of a lifetime's accumulated possessions, some with relatively little personal loss but with deep, traumatizing fears.

It was more than two years before I was comfortable enough to walk through my own home in the dark of the night—a practice I had often enjoyed while praying or meditating in the quiet of early mornings. But my struggle was nothing in comparison to the host who fled the city permanently, feeling so explosive an uncertainty could happen to them again. Nor did my trauma compare with those bereaved of a loved one, those suddenly out of work because the business was destroyed, or those with the long-term frustration of working through the rebuilding of a house shaken off its foundations.

The book of Revelation is meant for people like me, like you, *everyday* people who face *today first*. It's a book for people who need and deserve to get a stronger grip on *tomorrow* than interesting prophetic schemes or fascinating speculations can offer us. My words to you in this book are targeted at providing practical stuff for living *today first* and for your *immediate* tomorrow as well. I plan to discuss some vital insights into *the book of Revelation* that will, I believe, open the prophetic concepts in the book to a simpler, more practical understanding and use than most people expect when they read it casually.

And I *must* talk about the E Quake. Earth's last and greatest cataclysm is certain to come, and we deserve to understand *why* and *how*. But even in looking at *that* frightening and fascinating subject, I expect to have us unlock *the hope* it contains and *the help* it provides for understanding the Bible's closing book.

When the roar ceased that January morning and the heaviness of the moment was accentuated by the darkness in our bedroom,

I shouted, "Honey, are you there?" A soul-flooding relief swept over me as I heard my wife's voice, "I'm okay. Are you?" Where she had been flattened by the force of the quake, neither of the full-length closet door mirrors on one side had shattered or rained spears of glass onto her body, and the heavy six-foot-tall wooden chest on the other side didn't fall over as did so many furniture pieces throughout the house.

It wasn't the E Quake. It only raised the question, "Is this it?" This book is about not being devastated when it *does* come and about making life work in the meantime.

2

A HANDBOOK ON WORSHIP

Let me say it right up front—the book of Revelation will never make sense as a collection of prophecies until it is approached as a handbook on worship! But that isn't the usual focus we naturally come by. Why?

Because when we open Revelation's awesome look at earth's future, we quickly find ourselves caught up in its strange visions and seeming mysteries, for example:

- Multifaced beings chant around a heavenly throne (4:2–9).
- Varicolored horses gallop into the night as voices thunder their command to "Charge!" (6:1–8).
- Locustlike beings crawl the earth's surface with stingers in their tails that induce no end of agony in the earthlings they strike (9:1–10).

11

- A seven-headed, ten-horned monster rises out of the sea and is given global control by a dragon (13:1–19).
- The monster, the dragon, and a two-horned lamb belch out demonic frogs that create political turmoil and global warfare (16:13–14).
- A blood-drunken, scarlet-and-purple-clad harlot straddles a monster and rides forth, sexually manipulating world politicians and murdering church leaders (17:1–6).

It's just too much! The sweep of the scenario, with the mix of mystery and monstrosity in its cast of characters, commands our attention. The visions so completely become the point that we can miss "the point"—that is, the Vision Giver.

We shouldn't, however, because right at the front the fuller title of the book gives it away, announcing the book's primary purpose. Read it: the Revelation of Jesus Christ. It's not just a book about prophetic stuff, but a message from the Ultimate Prophet—the very Word of God Himself, showing us the glories of His person, the power behind His purpose, and the promises underwriting His program.

Revelation isn't an invitation to speculation. It is a summons to adoration—a call to focus on the glory of the Giver—because Revelation is a gift. It came first from the hand of Jesus to His trusted servant, John; then He intended to "unveil" the message (that's what Revelation means!). It's Jesus' desire to open our understanding, to make all that's in this book understandable and applicable. That happens best in an atmosphere of a heart that acknowledges the man Jesus of Nazareth, completely and worthily, as the Son of God—the magnificent Savior, Lord, and King that He is.

We need to establish this fundamental fact about the book of Revelation. I didn't invent it. There is no room for debate about it. The content of the book clearly shouts the fact. But too seldom is it even on the agenda in studies of Revelation, much less discussed as one of the keys to unlocking its richness. Here it is: to unlock its wealth, we must approach Revelation as a handbook on worship, not only as a collection of prophecies.

TAKING HOLD OF KEY #1

This worship focus wasn't something I recognized at first. Even though it becomes obvious when it is pointed out, the overwhelmingly dramatic nature of Revelation's pictures in prophecy too easily blocks our focus. Our Western-world mind-set is also far too inclined to separate intellectual pursuits from spiritual passion. Without meaning to, we may come to Revelation hoping so much to gain "insight into the future," "a grasp of things to come," "more knowledge about Jesus' second coming," that we miss Jesus Himself. However worthy those expectations, let me point the way with worship expectations. If that can take place, I guarantee that Revelation will open up in every way. It's basic. If we see the Lord, we'll see the lessons.

My personal breakthrough in penetrating the wealth of Revelation (as compared with the habit of "wondering" about it) came when I discovered two keys. We'll look at the second key later: the instructional key that relates to the E Quake and unlocks the structure of Revelation and brings its content into clearer arrangement. But we must start with the incarnational key, which relates to the spirit of worship that breathes through the whole of this book. To lay hold of the key of worship in our study and use of this book is to discover a transforming dynamic that will work for us in these ways: making it powerful in us (filling us with the Holy Spirit), and making it practical for us (enabling us to live in wisdom).

Come with me into and through the pages of the whole of this book. Let's survey its entirety to see the worship priority and to welcome the spirit of worship into our reading and examination of Revelation's pages. There are five essential principles regarding worship: (1) it begins with seeing the King; (2) it taps heaven's Supplier of health; (3) it aligns us with the throne; (4) it unlocks the release of divine deliverance; and (5) it will theme our eternal celebration.

1. WORSHIP BEGINS WITH SEEING THE KING

The centerpiece of the opening chapter of Revelation is Jesus—Jesus seen revealing Himself in the glory and splendor of His Royal Majesty. I want you to take a more detailed look at the beauty and implications of this visitation of our Savior as He lovingly went to the tortured setting of His apostle John. But for a moment right now, capture a sense of the opening summons to worship that Revelation's first chapter offers us.

Perhaps in all the Bible, this may be the most eloquent expression of the glory of Christ's majesty as our resurrected and ascended Lord and King. The elements of that glory and majesty are depicted in the portrait of the Master that John described:

> [I saw] One like the Son of Man, clothed with a garment down
> to the feet and girded about the chest with a golden band. His
> head and hair were white like wool, as white as snow, and His

eyes like a flame of fire; His feet were like fine brass, as if refined in a furnace, and His voice as the sound of many waters; He had in His right hand seven stars, out of His mouth went a sharp two-edged sword, and His countenance was like the sun shining in its strength. (Rev. 1:13–16)

The detail with which John described Jesus' appearance is not merely provided for the sake of color; it contains a message that John wanted to relay. Every feature of the Savior seen in this photograph is laden with significance, and John's audience would have understood each one.

His voice sounding like the thunder of a thousand waterfalls is an unmistakable statement that the Word is irresistibly alive and still speaking above the din of history.

His garment draping the full length of His body is the clothing of a Master, not the shorter garment of a servant. The statement: He who came in humility to serve, to seek, and to save is now enthroned on high as the Owner of creation.

His chestband woven of pure and refined gold is a regal ornamentation, in this case evidencing the purity and perfection that are the hallmarks of this King's rule.

His head and hair radiate that a mantle of the shekinah glory of God almighty rests upon Him.

His eyes are ablaze with a mix of the warmth and tenderness of the love of God, and the inescapable discernment and penetrating insight of the All-Knowing One.

His feet are a study in authority, for throughout the Scriptures, things "underfoot" are under the rule of the one whose feet are positioned over whatever is being referenced. The mention of their being bronzed, as though fired with the tempering power of flame, describes for us the feet that endured the flame of Calvary's suffering, being nailed to the cross, but are now in dominion above hell's dark power (Eph. 1:20–23).

His mouth and His hand express the sword of God's truth—the Holy Scriptures of promise and power that can slash and slay the adversary; and the Church's leaders (compare v. 16 and v. 20), those commissioned to train and lead the Church in spiritual warfare, taking "the sword of the Spirit, which is the word of God" (Eph. 6:17).

No wonder John fell down as though he had been struck by a bolt of lightning!

John's posture was one of abject worship. The book of Revelation opens with the account of a man at worship, prostrate before more than a vision: this is the Victor! Whatever struggle ensues, the Lord of glory is seen before and above it all. Don't bother to study Revelation until you capture this picture of the Revealer. This book will never be understood by analysts, but it can be grasped by worshipers. We could all afford to be prostrated before Jesus, voluntarily saying as we bow very, very low, "I worship You, almighty One. There is none like You!"

And don't miss this point: through worship, John made a choice. He might have been dominated by the oppressive circumstances surrounding him. Instead, he refused to be obstructed by those who opposed him as he bowed before the One who chose him.

Are you ever tempted to bitterness or rancor, to discouragement or despair, driven by those who oppose or oppress you? Seeing the King and worshiping Him can turn a victim mind-set to a victor's expectancy.

2. Worship Taps Heaven's Supplier of Health for the Body's Weakness

Notably, most of the several features of Jesus' person—each descriptive of attributes true to His magnificent character and throne—are repeated at some point in the second and third chapters of Revelation. The presumed point of understanding is that if Jesus is worthy of worship for these qualities that are present in Him, then the Church's worship is the pathway to remedy the Church's problems.

In this book, as we walk through the rich realities that Revelation 2 and 3 open to our understanding, we witness the sorry and the sordid, the unholy and the unhealthy, the perplexing and the problematic—all trying to steal the soul of Christ's Church. But at each point where He indicates need, we find that He is present to be the supply, out of the richness of His own person. Jesus, not methods, is the answer to any weakness present among His people.

Take, for example, the problem of financial need common in churches. Nothing could be more practical, and such need is most often present as a withered condition because of human neglect, unawareness, or outright disobedience in the fundamental worship practice of giving. In contrast to this, let me share a story. It demonstrates a wonderful model for solving financial shortage in the Church's life. I saw it in the ministry of my friend Jerry Cook years ago.

Jerry and his wife, Barbara, were then serving as senior pastors of the East Hill Foursquare Church in the Portland, Oregon, area. The thriving growth they were experiencing was, at one point, met with real financial challenges. With pressing need in the local budget, the pastor was faced with a problem: how to meet the missions obligations. In brief, the shortfall was threatening the fulfillment of the church's efforts at outreach. The temptation to take care of the church's need first was obvious. It was a reasonable argument: if the church didn't overcome its own difficulties, there wouldn't be a church to send funds to in the future.

At that point the Holy Spirit moved on Pastor Cook, who told me, "I sensed Him calling us to a test of faith; crowding me to believe that our financial solutions would not be found in preserving ourselves, but in worshiping our Savior—the Lord of the harvest. I felt Him calling us to present an offering that sowed abundantly into the need of others—trusting that God would multiply back to us that 'sowing,' underwriting our own needy circumstance by His grace, in contrast to our works."

With that conviction, Jerry called the congregation to worship by giving away, applying the principle taught in 2 Corinthians 8–9 where impoverished congregations gave greatly, notwithstanding their own financial stress. The story ends with what is probably an unsurprising surprise: the Lord abounded resource to answer the local need! God's bounty responded in more-than-adequate sufficiency, which came in, rebounding over the head of the young worshiping-through-giving-away-in-Christ's-name-and-love congregation.

As plain and direct as that testimony is, it's a practical teaching and a marvelous illustration of this principle: worship—in any of its worthy expressions—holds the solution to the sick or problem-beset church.

3. WORSHIP ALIGNS US WITH THE HEAVENLY THRONE

Revelation 4 is an invitation into the throne room of heaven. The indescribable scene includes John's effort at describing the cherubim—the "living creatures" situated nearest God's heavenly seat of universal authority. Let me tell about a powerful principle that the Holy Spirit used this chapter's setting to show me.

Just before I began pastoring The Church on the Way, one of the primary turning points in my life took place. It happened when I was at a conference where the Holy Spirit used a message on Acts 13 to stir my heart. The text was from the opening verses: "As they ministered to the Lord [a description of the church at worship] and fasted, the Holy Spirit said, 'Now separate to Me Barnabas and Saul for the work to which I have called them [an introduction to the church in evangelism]'" (v. 2).

Only a few months later, Anna and I came to our new pastorate, and at once, I sought to begin applying this principle: to teach the people that if we would prioritize worshiping the Lord, the Holy Spirit would move with a dynamic release of the spirit of evangelism.

The following two years, as we set ourselves as a congregation to live out an open, forthright, unconformed-to-this-world worship style as a people, there was a remarkable visitation of God's presence among us. Immediately, a remarkable increase began to take place in the number of people making decisions for Christ. Most surprising to me was how this was taking place, even without my focusing my messages on evangelism.

I was sure what was happening was the fruit of our prioritizing worship, for as we did, the Holy Spirit was clearly rewarding us with a wonderful sense of the presence of God descending upon the congregation. In that atmosphere, souls regularly came to Christ; a sense of "kingdom come" was marked in our midst.

It was there, in that season of blessing that has not concluded to this day, that an unusual experience provided me with a perspective on Revelation 4, which seemed to account for why the King comes so majestically wherever He is worshiped. I will describe my unusual experience in great detail in Chapter 5. For now, let me simply say that following the experience the Holy Spirit settled the following points of understanding into my soul:

- In each biblical description of God's throne, two things are mentioned: His glory and the presence of these unusual angelic beings (Isa. 6; Ezek. 1; Rev. 4).
- The positions of the four angelic beings are central to the throne—in immediate proximity to it, and round about the throne, that is, at four points closely surrounding it (Rev. 4:6).
- These creatures lead and stimulate praise, and they seem to seek to draw all the earth into chorus with their worship of the Creator (Isa. 6:3).
- As a congregation, we had set ourselves to be a people of continued praise and worship, who honor God's Word and glorify God's Son. And the Bible says that God is enthroned upon those praises (Ps. 22:3).

With those thoughts converging, with an incredibly precious sense of His teaching me, the Holy Spirit helped me to see a magnificent reality I don't think I would ever have grasped otherwise. I saw that in a wonderful way, in the invisible realm, the congregation's worship had brought our tiny house of worship into biblical alignment with the throne of God. Our commitment to worship had aligned us with God's address.

Thus, the wonderful sense of "kingdom come," which was so remarkably at work in transforming believers and drawing others to Jesus, was not due to a human attempt to get God to work, but simply that God's ruling presence—seated on His throne of all power—was not so much here as that with our praises, we had entered there! From Revelation 4, I was assisted to see how the praises and worship of God's people can establish an alignment with His throne that, in effect, actually puts Him in their midst in grace and power. As James put it, "Humble yourselves in the sight of the Lord . . . Draw near to God and He will draw near to you" (4:10, 8).

The book of Revelation points the way to the throne. Whether it is the worship of an individual, a family, a small group, or a congregation, a commitment to align with that throne through humility and sustained worship can open the way to "kingdom come." The splendor of God's working is not the result of the size of a crowd, the measure of an individual's or group's renown, or the achievement of human efforts. "All power" flows from His throne, and worship is the one way of approach and of welcoming the One in whom "all power in heaven and earth" is vested.

4. WORSHIP UNLOCKS THE RELEASE OF DIVINE DELIVERANCE

Another dynamic that began to infuse our congregation's life was born when the Holy Spirit called us to an ongoing assignment as regular intercessors for our nation. The understanding and atmosphere of perceived and received responsibility, essential if intercessory prayer is to be sustained, have been nourished by the spirit of worship. The book of Revelation conveys this concept in a dramatic way.

As with each of the passages mentioned in this chapter, significant details of the portions of Revelation will be elaborated later, but here I'm only mentioning their relevance to the theme of worship. Think with me, please, about the whole interior portion of the book—chapters 5–16.

Beginning with the worship scenes in Revelation 4–5, we enter the unfolding of the E Book—the scroll that, being opened, releases the sequences of the seven seals, seven trumpets, and seven bowls. An understanding of these activities is central to unlocking our understanding of Revelation, and we will come to that.

However, the evident place of worship, preceding the initiating of each sequence of judgments, poses a manifest truth to us regarding the role of worship. Worship is a key to unleashing God's operative works of deliverance. The evidence for this principle is in three passages—each of which precedes the opening of the book's next recorded series of prophesied judgments.

The worship of the redeemed host, honoring the Lion-Lamb who receives the scroll, sets forward the process of unsealing the sealed book—a process we will come to see as the means by which this old world is to be delivered from its ancient bondage (Rev. 5:8–14).

After the first six seals are broken, the seventh seal (which contains the seven trumpets within its scope) is not broken until we read of another megaburst of high praise and worship before the throne of almighty God. We witness a grand troop of those saved from throughout the nations of the whole earth, glorifying God (Rev. 7:9–12):

Amen! Blessing and glory and wisdom,
Thanksgiving and honor and power
    and might,
Be to our God forever and ever. Amen.

The result: chapters 8–9 record the sounding of the first six trumpets released to carry out their works of judgment as earth's deliverance proceeds.

The climaxing series of judgments—the seven bowls of God's wrath, which ensue with the sounding of the seventh trumpet—takes place only pursuant upon great, triumphant worship. Revelation 15:1–4 declares the glorious ways of God, concluding with the words, "[Now] Your judgments have been manifested."

The significance of this cluster of observations is that they confront today's believers with the fallacy of any notion that the church can program spiritual breakthrough. *Redemptive entry* is the term I like to use to describe what God does when His people invite Him to act today—to move in spiritual power, to overwhelm the powers of darkness by His sovereign might, to display His works of grace in every way to the glory of His Son. All these are actions of judgment against the powers of hell and deliverance dealt in behalf of those who receive His grace. It is our wisdom to learn from the revealed words of Revelation: God's mightiest works of power and deliverance are related in their release of the presence of the spirit of worship and praise among His people.

5. WORSHIP WILL THEME OUR ETERNAL CELEBRATION

The ultimate satisfaction thoughtful believers receive when reading and rereading the book of Revelation is seeing tomorrow's promise. The climax of God's grace will bring the complete and consummate fulfillment of His own people being with Him forever.

Shouts of triumphant praise roll like thunder as the great feast of the redeemed begins: "Alleluia! Salvation and glory and honor and power belong to the Lord our God! . . . Praise our God, all you His servants and those who fear Him, both small and great!" (Rev. 19:1, 5). In this same scene, John described hearing the voice of a great multitude, like a torrent of waters, saying, "Alleluia! For the Lord God Omnipotent reigns! Let us be glad and rejoice and give Him glory" (Rev. 19:6–7). The heavenly banquet has begun, and eternity's glories are beginning to unfold. We read: "Behold, the tabernacle of God is with men, and He will dwell with them, and they shall be His people. God Himself will be with them and be their God" (Rev. 21:3).

Here is the unfolding of the era of earth's history as we know it into the eternal graces we can hardly imagine, flowing forward with joy of endless fellowship and the intimacy of eternal worship.

Revelation begins and ends with worship. It is neither formulated by liturgical requirements nor manipulated by religious mandates. It is spontaneous, dynamic, explosive, and glorious. It bursts forth from created beings who have never fallen and from redeemed people who have been rescued from their fall.

And it is all centered on Jesus the Savior and glorifying to God the Father.

As we proceed through the Revelation, be open to the same Holy Spirit of worship in your soul and expressed through your whole being.

It's the heart of Revelation. And it will cause Revelation to unfold in your heart.

3   WHEN YOU FEEL YOU'RE AT THE END

REVELATION 1:1–20

Too often people study the book of Revelation from a sensationalized or speculative approach. I think you will be excited with me to learn more about the prophecies of this book, but I also think we can apply their practicality right now in our current circumstances.

> The Revelation of Jesus Christ, which God gave Him to show His servants—things which must shortly take place. And He sent and signified it by His angel to His servant John, who bore witness to the word of God, and to the testimony of Jesus Christ, to all things that he saw. Blessed is he who reads and those who hear the words of this prophecy, and keep those things which are written in it; for the time is near. John, to the seven churches which are in Asia: Grace to you and peace

from Him who is and who was and who is to come, and from the seven Spirits who are before His throne, and from Jesus Christ, the faithful witness, the firstborn from the dead, and the ruler over the kings of the earth. To Him who loved us and washed us from our sins in His own blood, and has made us kings and priests to His God and Father, to Him be glory and dominion forever and ever. Amen. Behold, He is coming with clouds, and every eye will see Him, even they who pierced Him. And all the tribes of the earth will mourn because of Him. Even so, Amen. "I am the Alpha and the Omega, the Beginning and the End," says the Lord, "who is and who was and who is to come, the Almighty." (Rev. 1:1–8)

My wife, Anna, and I have a collection of pictures that we have intentionally placed in a rather inconspicuous location, although people would probably enjoy seeing them. We didn't want people to enter my office or our house and suddenly be confronted by pictures of me and Anna with well-known people. I don't fault people who prominently display these types of pictures, but I felt that for me it could seem too much like name-dropping.

Along with these pictures are five framed letters. Three letters are from presidents, and two are from people who are known throughout the world. We especially treasure these letters because they were written specifically for us and they say some very affirming, nice things. The letters contain a personal word and words of commendation, which are very humbling and deeply meaningful.

I mention them as we begin because far more treasured is the personal letter that we are preparing to study. The book of

Revelation is a personal letter from Jesus to His Church. And what could be more treasured than a letter from Jesus? Especially when we are faced with things that undermine our confidence and sometimes the stability of our circumstances. Our character may not be attacked, but our sense of ease with where we are standing in life may be disturbed. Stuff happens. This week was filled with examples of what I'm talking about here.

Anna and I prayed with a young woman whose husband is just about to trash his family and run headlong into a divorce for no valid reason whatsoever other than a horrific entrapment—emotionally and mentally—by the Internet. His situation is absolutely characteristic of the insanity of our times.

This week, a couple in our church learned that one member of their family murdered another member of their family. They are servant-oriented, creative people, who are devoted to the Lord and using their gifts for His glory. And they are very effective in their own arena in the professional community. They have been stunned by the murder. There was no logical explanation for what happened—if there ever is an explanation for murder. There was no alcoholism or drug addiction or anything along those lines. It just happened. It exploded out of nowhere and burst upon the family.

Also this week, I was contacted by a dear man who had launched into a project with all of his heart, the maximum of his skill, and the wise counsel of others, but the enterprise collapsed in front of him. Upon close examination, the cause of the collapse was found to be a sorry oversight on his part. It was not a classic failure or a colossal action of some kind of folly. His great dreams were confirmed and launched, but a key component was forgotten. And I lamented the outcome for the man; I felt the pain in his voice.

A young woman whose husband was about to ruin their home, a couple facing a murder in the family, the collapse of a great vision—things happen. Whether you have been through such severe trials, you have at some time felt that you were at the end.

A LETTER TO YOU AND ME

This letter is given to the servants of Jesus. It is a letter to you and to me. John was encountered by Jesus, and he wrote, "The Revelation of Jesus Christ, which God gave to Him to show His servants—things which must shortly take place. And He sent and signified it by His angel to His servant John" (Rev. 1:1). John was simultaneously the amanuensis, the secretary or the stenographer who took down the letter, and the mailman who delivered it.

The Lord approached John where he was. It is a picture of circumstances so like ours that we can identify with him, and it shows much of the character and person of Jesus. But it is a very, very personal letter.

I want to fix that in our minds because it is going to be a great challenge, believe me, for us to capture all the prophetic significance of the book of Revelation and also gain what is often overlooked—the personal implications in practical ways for our lives.

Although the book of Revelation often becomes an object of sensation or speculation, when I look at the circumstances in which He presented it, I have no doubt whatsoever that Jesus never intended that for one split second. He was not writing to His people to tell them, "Here's a whole bunch of stuff you can guess about until I come again. It will be kind of fun to figure out which chart is right." More likely, He said, "I want to tell you a bunch of things that will make your life work in the middle of a world that has every kind of challenge you can imagine, and I want you to see the victory through it and beyond it. I want you to know that I am there when you feel you're at the end." That applies to the end of time or the end of your rope today.

This passage of Scripture identifies the reason that Jesus revealed Himself. The book of Revelation is not a revelation of "stuff"; *it is a revelation of Jesus*. It is not a revelation of information; *it is a revelation of Jesus*. It is not a revelation of prophecies; *it is a revelation of Jesus*.

We read in the first verse, "The Revelation of Jesus Christ, which God gave Him to show His servants." It is of Him, and it is from Him. That is why it opens with the disclosure of traits of His person that are manifest in a marvelous vision that John recorded. We are looking at Jesus.

As we study the whole book of Revelation, it is easy to become disjointed in our perspective and concentrate on episodes and activities in the book. Mention the book of Revelation and you are less likely to hear somebody ask, "What did you capture of new things about Jesus in that book?" than to hear somebody ask, "What do you think 666 really is? Who are the two witnesses? When is the Rapture going to happen?" The focus of the book is on Jesus, and we must focus on Him.

At the beginning of the book, Jesus made clear His purpose. He revealed Himself, first and foremost, to help us keep things in perspective. The revelation was given that He might show "things which must shortly take place . . . for the time is near" (1:1, 3).

I know we read those words and say, "I believe Jesus is coming soon, but He wrote those words centuries ago. It seems that it is a relative thing. John thought He was coming, but He didn't come then. Paul thought He was coming, but He didn't come then. And people in the last generation thought He was coming. I think He is coming, and I really feel He is coming in my life, but who knows?"

Please hear me, loved one. The Lord wants you to gain a heavenly perspective. Until it grips your heart, you will forever be driven by the nature of life lived in the time-space continuum. Life lived in the time-space continuum tends to stampede you and distress you when pressure comes on you because you figure this is the way life is going to be.

By saying "things which must shortly take place," Jesus was saying, "I want you to see that whatever you are at the end of, whatever the tough stuff is, whatever the struggle is, whatever you are going through is brief in comparison with what your life is ultimately about."

Dear one, your life is not ultimately about your present financial or domestic stress. Your life is not ultimately about . . . I can finish that sentence a dozen ways. I am not suggesting that you become passive about life's realities. I am not suggesting that the Lord is indifferent to problems. He was saying, "I want you to see Me and to see that whatever you are going through is not what your life is ultimately about! Underscore it in your mind! It is important, it has to be dealt with, and I will move with you through it." And we will see how graciously He does because He disclosed more than this preliminary statement. But He wants to help you and me keep things in perspective.

Jesus came to say to us, "I am here in your interest, and I am committed to seeing you through it all." He offered an incredible incentive: "Blessed is he who reads." You want a blessing? Keep reading this. Staying in this book will keep your eyes above it all.

Jesus signed it Himself: "He sent and signified it . . . to His servant John" (1:1). The signature of Jesus on the book is of no small significance. It means He was saying, "This is personal to you, from Me." And He was saying, "I am putting My name on it. I am endorsing everything I have said here."

Many years ago Anna and I were offered a very prestigious pulpit. It was an incredible situation and a marvelous opportunity. We didn't go because we didn't feel the call of God. But it had everything that a young pastor could dream of as a possibility for his future. They even said, "We are authorized to offer you a blank check; you name your salary." Most people would think, *This must be of God!* Well, it wasn't. And those people weren't trying to buy us out because they knew we had more character than that. They were basically asking us to set what we felt would be an appropriate salary. What made the offer credible wasn't the blank check. It was knowing the financial strength of the church and the character of the congregation. It had all the resources that could have justified just about any number I wanted to put in there.

The point is that Jesus was endorsing something for us when He said: "Rest your life on this, for I am the Life Giver. I will support you. I am the Resurrected One, the First and the Last. Death can't keep Me down, and when you come to the end, it can't keep you down, either. I am going to see you through it all. I have made you kings and priests unto God." There is a promise of dominion as long as we walk in worship. We are kings who war with victory and priests who, through worship, draw the authority to function as kings (1:6).

The Message Revealed

The content of the message proceeds from there. From verse 9 through verse 20, John described an encounter. The encounter gives us the message Jesus revealed. It is a message with six parts.

1. Jesus' Love Can Find You Anywhere

The first part of the message we derive from John's words in Revelation 1:9: "[I] was on the island that is called Patmos." John explained that he was there because he was under persecution from the Roman government. Notice the phrase "the island that is called Patmos." There is something particularly significant about those words. They tell us that Patmos was not a well-known location. It has become one of the best-known places in the world, however.

Patmos, a Greek island in the Aegean Sea, is a dot on the face of this planet. It was a nowhere place, a Roman penal colony less than four miles square. And of the little island, even then in a world much smaller in terms of people knowing the scope of this planet, John said, "An island called . . ." You say that only when people haven't heard of what you're talking about. It has become so famous in our time that cruise ships with no real interest in Patmos for the history that we Christians observe still go there. It is a nice port and an interesting spot in the Aegean. People know of Patmos today, but they didn't when John delivered this letter.

Jesus was visiting John, and John wanted to make a point. He was not just imparting interesting information. He was saying, "This message reveals the Lord Jesus saying, 'You can never be in so forsaken a place that My love won't seek and find you.'" That is the heart of the message, which applies to you, even if you feel that you are in a place called Confusion or Despair, or that you are isolated on an island called Rejection. The Lord spoke to him, and John reported, "Jesus came to me when I was on an island off in the middle of nowhere. That's the kind of Jesus we serve."

2. YOU CAN TRANSCEND ANY CIRCUMSTANCE

John added, "I was in the Spirit on the Lord's Day, and I heard behind me a loud voice, as of a trumpet" (1:10). This is the second part of Jesus' message.

John was in a penal colony, and he was under the scepter of the world's imperial power of that time, Rome. No escape and no circumstance could alter that. He was under the control, under the heel of the Roman Empire. And John said, "I was there at the end of the world and at the end, apparently, of anything I could do or become with no way out by reason of the power and authority of human control. And on this day I transcended that, I went into the Spirit on the Lord's Day. I might have been on Patmos, but I want to tell you about a day that I got in the Spirit."

Loved one, whenever you feel that you are at the end, you can identify your surroundings and circumstances and suppose they are the limits, or you can transcend those limits by coming before Father God and saying, "Father God, I worship You." By getting in the Spirit, you can transcend any circumstance. It isn't just a matter of "happy talk" or trying to get an emotional kick and feeling better about it. It is a matter of recognizing that you can move into the realm of the Spirit through worship.

"I was in the Spirit on the Lord's Day." There are two ways to interpret that statement and John was probably referring to both. "On the Lord's Day" is a phrase that would have meant then, as it means today, the first day of the week, the Lord's Day. Jesus sanctified the first day of the week through His resurrection. John probably had no one to worship with, but he began to worship the Lord.

"On the Lord's Day" is also a phrase that dramatically reflects throughout Scripture the day of God's judgment and visitation, the day that God will come to change things, the day that He will come to crush His enemies and to release His own. John was going to capture a vision of that whole thing, through the processes of which would come the eventual entry of God's delivering power over this whole planet and the eventual triumph of His people.

"I was in the Spirit on the Lord's Day." I love hearing people proclaim, "I was in the Spirit!" It lets you know that this is more than just a moment of the status quo. Something is going on in them, and I may sense that there is an emotional quality to it. So what? There is also a spiritual dynamism.

Loved ones, John was conveying what Jesus wants us to see in this verse: "You can never be in so bound a state that My Spirit can't lift your soul with hope. So, get in the Spirit."

3. JESUS IS THE REDEEMER OF CIRCUMSTANCES

Third, John said, "I heard behind me a loud voice, as of a trumpet, saying, 'I am the Alpha and the Omega, the First and the Last,' and, 'What you see, write in a book'" (1:10–11). Then Jesus told John to direct the book to the congregations that John had overseen.

In this statement, "I am the Alpha and the Omega," I suppose most people know that alpha and omega are the *A* and *Z* of the Greek alphabet. Jesus said, "I am the Alpha and the Omega, the First and the Last," coupled with phrases where He described His mission in the name of the One who was, who is, and who is to come. I like Eugene Peterson's translation from the Greek text: "THE GOD WHO IS, THE GOD WHO WAS, AND THE GOD ABOUT TO ARRIVE" (*The Message*).

Jesus is saying, "Your history can't be written until I have the last word." Jesus is the One who is the beginning. He is the Author and the Finisher of our faith. He is the Creator as well as the Consummator of all things. Between the creation and the consummation, He is the Redeemer of whatever you are going through. He is the *A* to *Z*, the Alpha and the Omega, the First and the Last. When you write down in the book wherever you are in the middle of whatever you are in what seems like the end, Jesus is telling you that is not the end of the story yet! He is saying, "I am going to write the end of your story, and I am going to write it *My* way, no matter what the circumstance." This merits a response of the spirit that says, "I am going to take that for me!"

When Jesus went to John personally, John wasn't proudly saying, "I had a personal visit from Jesus, and I am here at this local Christian banquet to tell you how I, the Apostle, heard from God." To the contrary, he said, "I, John, both your brother and companion in the tribulation" (1:9). In other words, "We go through tough stuff together, and I am just another member of the family. I want to tell you how Jesus treats members of the family." The only logic for John's reporting that was to declare the authority upon which he related what followed and to let us know the way that Jesus revealed Himself, how He revealed Himself, and what it is intended to mean to us. And it is intended to mean these things that I have summarized.

> Then I turned to see the voice that spoke with me. And having turned I saw seven golden lampstands, and in the midst of the seven lampstands One like the Son of Man, clothed with a garment down to the feet and girded about the chest with a golden band. His head and hair were white like wool, as white as snow, and His eyes like a flame of fire; His feet were like fine brass, as if refined in a furnace, and His voice as the sound of many waters; He had in His right hand seven stars, out of His mouth went a sharp two-edged sword, and His countenance was like the sun shining in its strength. And when I saw Him, I fell at His feet as dead. But He laid His right hand on me, saying to me, "Do not be afraid; I am the First and the Last." (Rev. 1:12–17)

In Revelation 1:12–17, John was writing in at least the eightieth year of his life; he might have been as old as ninety or ninety-five. As John wrote those words and described the encounter with Jesus, the last time he saw Jesus personally was on a hill outside Jerusalem, the Mount of Olives, in the year A.D. 30. Sixty years had passed since he *saw* Jesus. He obviously had had an ongoing relationship with Jesus in the years since then. John walked with the Savior.

The last time that John saw Jesus, who though resurrected was still there in the aftermath of Calvary, He blessed them there on the mountain. The agony points were manifest, wounds that He will carry throughout eternity, but in the ordinariness of His garb, the humanness of His presence in glorified humanity, there was a commonality of this earth.

Suddenly, John said, "I heard behind me a loud voice, as of a trumpet . . . then I turned." He described what he saw, though words seemed to fail him. He labored to come up with a description: "Eyes like fire . . . Oh, if you could have seen the way that His hair was . . ." He described the splendor of the majesty of the reigning Christ who, at the right hand of the throne of all power, is the Lord of all. Jesus said, "I am He who lives, and was dead, and behold, I am alive forevermore . . . I have the keys of Hades and of Death" (1:18). John looked at Him, was overcome, and fell down. John was overcome with a sense of the majesty of the Savior.

I believe there is great significance in this encounter because no one knew Jesus any better than John did. He was the disciple who, we might say, was the closest friend of the Savior in terms of a confidant during His earthly ministry. The most familiar person who had been with Him for years and who was there on the last occasion that He was seen on this earth turned to see Him and was overwhelmed.

4. JESUS IS CLOSER THAN YOU THINK

I hear a message of Jesus speaking to those of us who know Him well. This is the fourth part of His message. When we think we are at the end or when we move through life with its daily, weekly, and monthly trials the Lord says, "I know that you know Me." But I think the Lord is saying through this encounter with John: "You may think that you know Me well, but you haven't seen anything yet."

Loved one, Jesus calls to you in the midst of your circumstance when you feel you are at the end: "You lift up your head just a little higher because I am greater than you think, more powerful than you think, and closer than you think."

5. YOU CAN FIND YOUR SECURITY IN JESUS

In verses 15–20 there are two other noteworthy statements. When the Bible says that "His feet were like fine brass, as if refined in a furnace" (v. 15), the figure is intended to announce this: those feet once wounded have become feet of dominion. The figure of brass in the Scriptures regularly denotes strength, just as the tempering effect of the fire causes the metal to be prepared for what would become a shield or a guard of another part of the body for warfare, or what would become the brazen gates to defend a city. At that time in history brass that had been fired in a furnace depicted strength in a way that no other image did.

I couldn't help wondering as I thought about that last vision of Jesus as He went up to be with the Father. The last thing noticeable, perhaps as He disappeared into the fog bank, were the feet that had been pierced. And now John saw that the feet had a brazen quality. They were not brass feet; they were feet that appeared as brass. The glory and authority of the Savior who sits on the throne are evident, all principalities and powers under His feet, and He has called us to completeness in Him. He says that as you find your security in Him, those feet begin to manifest through you. And whatever of the serpentine or the scorpionlike attacks of the adversary, the Lord says you will crush the serpents and the scorpions under your feet. Walk in the trail of the One who has gone through the fire. And the fifth part of the message is this: going through the fire as He did, with Him, you discover what He found going through it.

I spoke with a young pastor recently who was facing tremendous difficulty because he felt forsaken. I called on him to rest his case with the Lord nonetheless. He wasn't angry with God; he just felt that he couldn't trust in Him. I reminded him that Jesus said, "My God, why hast Thou forsaken Me?" and only a few words later said, "Into Your hands I commend My Spirit."

In that moment of His greatest sense of aloneness came His greatest abandonment of trust and rest in the Father. When you go through the fires, no matter what causes you to say, "It seems to me, I am at the end, and God is not even around in this situation anymore," the Lord responds, "If you will abandon yourself and trust Me, then you will go through that fire, and you will find a pathway of dominion like My Son's." In this passage Jesus is saying, "There is nothing you face that is unanticipated by My plan or unsurpassed by My power."

That was what the Savior went through at the Cross. The Father's plan and the Father's power brought Him through. He says, "That's how My feet got this way. I want you to walk with Me and learn the same thing. There is never a plan to disregard or neglect you, no matter how alone or confused you feel in the midst of life. My plan transcends it, and My power will take you through it."

6. JESUS HAS HIS HAND ON YOU

With this, we come to the final part of His message. Verses 16 and 20 mention that in the Savior's right hand were stars. Those stars were people, but not stars as we think of them in terms of famous personalities. They were stars in the sense of the radiance invested in people of the kingdom of God. The radiance is intended to light the darkness of the world. We read in Philippians 2:15: "You may become blameless and harmless, children of God without fault in the midst of a crooked and perverse generation, among whom you shine as lights in the world." Stars in the night, "a thousand points of light," as one former president spoke of them, or ten thousand points of light, the Lord has millions of them.

John saw that hand with the stars, he fell before Jesus, and he said that He put "His right hand on me" (1:17). That is, just when Jesus seemed to be out of reach, He said, "I have you and your circumstances firmly in hand." That was what He was saying through that encounter with John.

We sing, "He's got the whole world in His hands." But the verses mention the baby in His hands, "you and me, brother, in His hands," and "you and me, sister, in His hands." Each of us—not a few special, select people—is in His hands.

This passage of Scripture tells us that this book of prophecy that we call the Revelation of Jesus Christ is intended to come not just to people who are talking about the ultimate end. That is of significance, though, especially in times like ours, especially in times when we talk about the Y2K millennium bug, and the questions and problems that come to people's minds in that environment. But whether there is anything else that seems to be an imminent problem in the world, we've got our own problems, and we feel that we are at the end. Whether it is the end of time or the end of our ropes, the Savior tells us, "I am here. I am here."

Jesus reassures you, "I am here, no matter how remote you seem to yourself or out of touch. No matter what you think I may have been like in times past, you haven't seen anything yet. I am here in the middle of your circumstance to put My hand on you, to show My glorious power, to walk you through the fire. I am here. I have come to show you that compared to what your life is ultimately about, this is only a brief time. I am going to take you through it." He doesn't say it is brief to tell you it is unimportant. He wants you to recognize that He is able to manage it right here, right now. Jesus is here.

The book of Revelation—let us enter it not as speculators on prophetic notions, but as participators in a daily life that for all of us may be being carried out in end times and that for each of us at various times may pose problems that seem like the end. Hear the Word of the Lord. We have the promise of His presence and the certainty of His victory in us because He is here.

4 | JESUS AND THE TERMINATOR

To the angel of the church of Ephesus write, "These things says He who holds the seven stars in His right hand, who walks in the midst of the seven golden lampstands: 'I know your works, your labor, your patience, and that you cannot bear those who are evil. And you have tested those who say they are apostles and are not, and have found them liars; and you have persevered and have patience, and have labored for My name's sake and have not become weary. Nevertheless I have this against you, that you have left your first love. Remember therefore from where you have fallen; repent and do the first works, or else I will come to you quickly and remove your lampstand from its place—unless you repent. But this you have, that you hate the deeds of the Nicolaitans, which I also hate. He who has an ear, let him hear what the Spirit says to the churches. To him who overcomes I will give to eat from the tree of life, which is in the midst of the Paradise of God.'" (Rev. 2:1–7)

LETTERS TO THE CHURCHES

The first letter embodies the pattern for all the letters to the churches. You will find these common denominators.

Each one is addressed to "the angel of the church" in a community in ancient Asia Minor. The Greek word *angelos* means "messenger" as well as "angel." Angels are messengers of God while people who bring the Word of God are messengers too. The word *angel* here applies to the leader of the local congregation. So it is addressed to the leader of the church—the messenger of the church.

The second thing in each letter is a disclosure of something of the person of Jesus: "These things says He who holds the seven stars in His right hand, who walks in the midst of the seven golden lampstands" (2:1). The lampstands represent the churches. We are told that at the end of chapter 1. Jesus was the One who was moving among the pastors and the churches. He was dealing with the leaders, and He was dealing with the body. A different trait of Jesus' person opens every letter. "These things says He who . . . ," and then it describes something about Jesus, which was taken from the way John saw Him in the vision in chapter 1.

The next thing in every letter is Jesus' statement: "I know your works." Five letters call the congregation to account for something that is being neglected or overlooked. The other two letters contain only approval.

Next, it uniformly says, "He who has an ear, let him hear." Seven times it says that.

Finally, it says that to those who overcome, who confront this and respond to it, there is a reward.

> And to the angel of the church in Smyrna write, "These things says the First and the Last, who was dead, and came to life: 'I know your works, tribulation, and poverty (but you are rich); and I know the blasphemy of those who say they are Jews and are not, but are a synagogue of Satan. Do not fear any of those things which you are about to suffer. Indeed, the devil is about to throw some of you into prison, that you may be tested, and you will have tribulation ten days. Be faithful until death, and I will give you the crown of life. He who has an ear, let him hear what the Spirit says to the churches. He who overcomes shall not be hurt by the second death.'" (Rev. 2:8–11)

A couple of years ago I had gone to my study area in our home, planning to turn on the ten o'clock news as I prepared for bed. I happened to be a little ahead of time, so I flipped the channel. The end of a movie was going on. It was horrible! It was absolutely terrifying! I had an idea of what the movie was, having seen trailers when the movie was being promoted two or three years earlier, but I wasn't positive because I hadn't seen it announced for television.

There was a creature that took any form it needed to get to the object of its antagonism. I didn't know the plot, but I saw a hideous, metallic kind of face and then a meltdown. I am talking about the character called the Terminator.

After I saw the hideous ending, I thought that someday I would talk to somebody about the story line behind the movie. I did, and I found out how the story goes. You may know the story, but it came to my mind because something in the plot of that film relates to this portion of Revelation.

There are two films. What I saw was the end of number two. Story number one has to do with a time in the future when there is a person who becomes the instrument of crushing evil and making things good for people. But a sinister force wants to control and dominate people and destroy them. To preempt this person in the future, to stop this from happening, the people behind the sinister force commission this being to go back to the past to head off the birth. In the first movie, the Terminator tries to kill the one who will be the mother of this child, and then in *Terminator 2*, another terminator tries to kill the person himself. The whole purpose is to terminate the possibility of the good force. That is *The Terminator* in brief.

I thought about the way this being takes many different forms to effectively stop what is intended to be a force that will break evil and will bring blessing to humanity. It is a perfect picture of the conflict in which the adversary seeks to pollute or distort the mind of the Church and preempt what the Lord wants to do in the Church so that it can be an instrument of deliverance and blessing to humanity.

Just as the Terminator takes on different forms in order to achieve his ends, there are different forms that confusion, evil, flesh, and devil take in order to stop the Church from being the Church. I want us to see Jesus confronting this.

This passage begins with a visitation. Sixty years after the birth of the Church, Jesus was walking among the churches. He had been present in a certain way, but here we see the very dramatic presence of Jesus saying, "I am He who walks among the seven golden lampstands."

The "lampstand" describes the light that the Church is meant to be in the darkness. Jesus, the Light of the World, ignited light in His people. And when Jesus talked about the churches, He was talking about His people. The churches are His people, you and me.

JESUS CONFRONTS TERMINATORS OF
THE LIFE OF THE CHURCH

These seven letters form a complete review of things that over the centuries have beset the Church. What happened in the first century was an effort of a terminating influence to stop the Church from being the Church, and Jesus confronted it. Many of those same things appear from generation to generation, and they appear within local congregations. Everything mentioned here in one way or another could appear in almost any church with 150 to 200 people. These things are potential terminators of the vital life of the Church. And Jesus came to confront them.

In His confrontation four things stand out. Let's move together through several texts of chapters 2 and 3.

1. THE SUBSTITUTION OF ACTIVITIES FOR PRIORITIES

This confrontation is with things proved to corrupt or disintegrate the Church's influence. The first one is the *substitution of activities for priorities*.

Listen to these words: "I know your works, your labor, your patience, and that you cannot bear those who are evil. And you have tested those who say they are apostles and are not, and have found them liars; and you have persevered and have patience, and have labored for My name's sake and have not become weary" (Rev. 2:2–3).

Jesus said, "You have been working for Me, you have been serving, you have been faithful to the Word of truth, you have been faithful to the things of value, and you have not wearied when time went by." You can hear the heart of the Savior saying, "You've done great!"

But then what? "Nevertheless I have this against you, that you have left your first love" (2:4).

This reminder is needed in all of life. People who study corporations that rise to a great place of success observe that they often plateau and lose their momentum or they absolutely lose their place and disintegrate. The dynamics that occasioned the rise to a place of effectiveness are forgotten and lost because the machinery, the bureaucracy, takes over and loses the vital life of the corporation.

This happens in homes and marriages where people go through the motions. They lose being close to one another. There are a myriad of ways that this could be applied, but Jesus said, "No matter how much you serve Me, how much work you do, how faithful you are in the performance of righteous things, don't lose your touch with Me."

If we lose touch with Jesus, we lose contact with the fountain of the Church's power. There is a loss of centering on the foundation that the Church is built on. The Church is built on Jesus. The Church draws the fountain of its life from Jesus.

Notice the repetition in several verses: "I know your works" (2:9, 13, 19; 3:8, 15). To those churches, He said, "I know your works, and you are doing good things."

To one, the busyness wasn't achieving anything good: "And to the angel of the church in Sardis write, 'These things says He who has the seven Spirits of God and the seven stars: "I know your works, that you have a name that you are alive, but you are dead . . . I have not found your works perfect before God"'" (3:1–2). An absolute barrenness had come. Even the works weren't worth that much.

Jesus repeatedly addressed the Church: "I know your works; I know your works." But He added, "Don't mistake activity for answering to your priorities."

One of the most dramatic illustrations of this will be when Jesus will stand before His own at the end of time and some people will be amazed to discover that they aren't included. They will come and plead their cases. Listen to what they will say because—hear me, loved one—what they will say is something that especially those of us of pentecostal and charismatic traditions would suppose to be the ultimate verifying evidence that they really had touch with God. Listen to what they will say: "Lord, have we not prophesied in Your name, cast out demons in Your name, and done many wonders in Your name?" And the Bible says that Jesus will say to them, "I never knew you; depart from Me" (Matt. 7:22–23). They had activity but no real relationship. Authority but no intimacy. We need transparency, respondency to Jesus.

I want to say something without creating an aura of suspicion. Dear one, don't make the mistake of supposing that just because a ministry appears to have power, it is sound. You may say, "Well, they talk in Jesus' name." The issue is, Are people drawn to Jesus, to love Jesus, to follow Jesus? Or do they get caught up in a trail of activity, however noble or mighty it may seem? "Have we not done many wonders in Your name?"

This passage then explains that the fountain of your power is your relationship with Jesus, not the dominion or authority you seem to be able to manifest in ministry. This is not an argument against dynamic ministry. It is not to create suspicion every time you see miracle power or dominion over the works of darkness. But probe farther than a momentary thrill, and don't stop by observing, "They seem so anointed." Is Jesus the center of it all? Not just His name being used, but are you drawn to Jesus, to love Jesus?

2. THE TOLERATION OF IMPURITY

The second thing that can terminate the life of the Church is the *toleration of impurity*.

Look at these verses:

> I have a few things against you, because you have there those who hold the doctrine of Balaam, who taught Balak to put a stumbling block before the children of Israel, to eat things sacrificed to idols, and to commit sexual immorality . . . Nevertheless I have a few things against you, because you allow that woman Jezebel, who calls herself a prophetess, to teach and seduce My servants to commit sexual immorality and eat things sacrificed to idols. And I gave her time to repent of her sexual immorality, and she did not repent. (2:14, 20–21)

Then read verse 24: "To you I say, and to the rest in Thyatira, as many as do not have this doctrine [the practice of

Jezebel], who have not known the depths of Satan." That is quite an interesting phrase, isn't it? What are the depths of Satan in the context of this Scripture, the warnings regarding Balaamism and Jezebelism? Let's talk about what they are and then deal with the expression "the depths of Satan."

Both Balaamism and Jezebelism refer to Old Testament characters. These names are used to depict that same spirit being expressed in local congregations. In neither case did it say it was true of everybody in the church. People were living, thinking, and responding that way because of influences being brought to bear upon them by supposed leaders who ought to have been trusted, but Jesus was saying, "No!" What was happening was analogous to the Old Testament influence of Balaam and Jezebel. In both cases they influenced people toward sexual immorality.

Now don't think that God or the Bible or I am prudish about sex. God has given us remarkable capacities for fulfillment in the sexual aspects of our personalities and our humanity. But the Lord has also given clear guidelines on the maximum of that fulfillment, and He has confined them to marriage. He did not give us these guidelines because He is narrow-minded. Human beings experience fulfillment when the relationship is built and grown in every aspect, not just the sexual. And God always wants the best for us.

Some people think this doesn't make any difference—that's Balaam—while others tell you—and this is where the depths of Satan come in—that this is really God's idea. In other words, immorality is God's idea. That seems inconceivable to our minds, but there are different ways that it comes into the human mind.

I want to briefly probe the meaning of "the depths of Satan." I define it this way: to consciously pursue impurity under the guise of having permission from God. I have no idea how many times in my years of pastoral ministry I have met people who felt they had some special dispensation or license from God to indulge themselves in areas of sexual inappropriateness. And I don't mean only sexual intercourse outside marriage. I am talking about the same thing Jesus talked about in the passage regarding the church at Thyatira. He addressed sexuality in terms of physical performance, and He talked about their minds and their hearts as well. He talked about how the mind and the heart become stolen by sexual immorality.

We live in a day of easy access to pornography and base and corrupt things through Internet resources, not to mention materials that may be purchased in profusion at so-called adult stores. The question is not, Do you love Jesus Christ, and are you a part of His Church? The question is, Is there a place in your mind, your heart, or your practice where you think that you have a certain license for occasional indulgence to a certain point and that it is okay because of the way you define it?

I don't want these comments to come across as "pile it on while the president's down," but we have a tragic and obvious example of this glaring in our faces nationally at the time of this writing. A man of obvious brilliance and intelligence says, "I didn't really know what you meant when you said 'sexual relationship.'" I am not trying to be funny, but no one really believes that. The point is, we live in a society that talks that way all the time, so much so that it can seep into our own suppositions.

Jesus confronted this vulnerability in the life of the Church because it will terminate the Church's dynamism. Let me tell you why.

To indulge yourself outside the biblical guidelines in terms of sexual behavior is to abandon yourself to demonic influence and thereby to be restricted in your capacities for what the Lord wants you to be. It may not damn your soul to hell, but it will certainly bring so much hell into your life that you won't do much good for heaven.

And it will adversely affect your confidence. You cannot log off an Internet site where you have just fed your mind trash and the next moment feel bold when an opportunity to be something for Jesus arises. You have been compromised in your soul. It has nothing to do with whether you really love the Lord and want to be an agent of His life. You are neutralized through residual condemnation and a sense of not being His. It terminates the power life of the Church.

That is the second thing that Jesus headed off—the toleration of impurity as immaterial and the notion that casual attitudes in this area are approvable.

3. THE FALLACY THAT MATERIAL SUCCESS IS SYNONYMOUS WITH BLESSING

The third thing that Jesus cited is the *fallacy that material success is synonymous with blessing.*

Look with me at 3:17: "Because you say, 'I am rich, have become wealthy, and have need of nothing'—and do not know that you are wretched, miserable, poor, blind, and naked." Listen to the Lord now. He said you are talking about doing well, but you are absolutely struck with poverty.

In contrast, look at 2:9: "I know your works, tribulation [that means you are going through a lot of troubles], and poverty (but you are rich)." Isn't that interesting?

The facts were poverty, yet Jesus said, "You are rich." Others said, "We're really doing great!" yet He said, "You are naked."

This does not mean that anyone who has financial resources falls into the category of coming under His correction or that there is special nobility in being poor. He was talking about the deception that supposes that material success is synonymous with the blessing of the Lord. I trust that no one will mistake my spirit in making the following observation.

More than a decade ago the Church of Jesus Christ was absolutely shaken and embarrassed before the eyes of the entire planet by reason of the scandals surrounding two television ministries. Most notable was the ministry of PTL and Jim and Tammy Bakker.

I want to jump ahead of myself a moment. Jim Bakker was my pulpit guest in our church after he was released from prison. Jim confessed his horrendous failure to the body of Christ, and he apologized for the way that he embarrassed the Church before the eyes of the world. He had compromised his leadership and paid a debt to society with nearly seven years in prison. He was my friend before he went in prison, he was my friend while he was in prison, and he was my friend when he came out. Jim had come to reckon with the fact that, as the title of his book about the situation echoes, "I was wrong." But it was too late.

I have never made a whole lot out of this because it can sound as though I arrogate something of superiority to myself, and I don't feel that way. I grieve over what happened. I rejoice that Jim has come through the ordeal. It is still lamentable. All that happened—and the horrible price paid—was because of the notion that material success is synonymous with blessing.

From the middle seventies to the late seventies, I was invited to participate in PTL many times. I went there, spoke at seminars, and was on broadcasts. In the late seventies, I decided I wasn't going there anymore. I did two times because of special circumstances where I felt I should. I could see a storm brewing, and many people, including me, warned them. But nobody would listen because of the attitude that "this must be God because look at how this towering empire is happening."

Dear one, I'm not bringing up the past to make us look righteous and somebody else look bad. I am telling you that the Church of Jesus Christ has proved in our lifetimes, in the last decade or two, how vulnerable it is to submitting to this terminator of vital life.

And right now the same thing is happening. I don't know who you are, but you may be charmed by scenes that you see in Christian ministry and you say, "That must be the blessing. Just look at the splendor of it all!" I am not telling you that because something is marvelous and splendid, it is necessarily wrong, but its splendor doesn't verify it. And that is important.

We need to come to terms with the fact that material success is not synonymous with blessing. Let that sink in deep. And let us recognize the "me-ism" that occupies the Church. As long as everything looks great and wonderful, we're on the sailboat to glory. This is an important point of warning. Come to a fourth one with me, please.

4. THE PLACEMENT OF RELIGIOUS SYSTEMS THAT REMOVE GRACE AND GLORY

The fourth confrontation of Jesus is the *placement of religious systems that remove grace and glory*. Twice He mentioned a group called the Nicolaitans (2:6, 15), and twice He used the phrase "the synagogue of Satan" (2:9; 3:9). Let me explain them.

Read these verses:

> This you have, that you hate the deeds of the Nicolaitans, which I also hate . . . Thus you also have those who hold the doctrine of the Nicolaitans, which thing I hate. (2:6, 15)

I was speaking to a group of about eight hundred men near Albany, Oregon. My topic was the flow of the life of the Lord through a person, which causes the fulfillment of the grace of God to bring about fruitfulness and doing good for other people. This fruitfulness happens through you because you are nothing more than what you were made to be in the love of God and under the life and power of Jesus. It is not a matter of getting up in the morning and deciding that you have to do fifteen things to serve God. You get up and do what you do, and the life of Jesus flows through you because what you were made to be is being realized.

I stepped down so that I would be at floor level with the group. I wanted to emphasize a point about Nicolaitanism. Nicolaitanism is based on the two words that comprise the word—*nikaos* and *laos*. Bible commentators say it represents a hierarchy that has to do with the people who are up on the platform or the people who hold office in the church. It is the belief that these are the truly important ones, and the rest are peons. It is the notion that the Church is an institution and the people who head the institution and hold the power are really the ones who are important to God. They are the ones who have the real contact. They are the "movers and shakers." However, that is not what the Church is about.

Nikaos is the Greek word for "to conquer" or "to dominate." *Laos* is the word for "people"; we get the word *laity,* "the people," from it. The Nicolaitans dominated the people in such a way that they had become a substitute for their ministry. The people didn't really have ministry; the people funded the projects and listened to the leader and didn't do much.

I put it this way to the group: "Here, sitting in this room, is somebody with grease ground into your skin so that you can never really get it out. You spend your life under cars or trucks. You are a mechanic, and you work constantly in that arena. You do that most days of your life, and you love it. You love working there. And I want to tell you something about why you do. It isn't just because it is something you like.

"Listen, brother, you like that because God made you to do that kind of thing. That's what you are; you're a mechanic. And you are a mechanic God made to be a mechanic. Every day you go to work, it is not a matter of doing some great thing for God but just going and being God's man as a mechanic in that place. Then if something comes up where the Lord wants to use you in some way that we call spiritual ministry, fine, but while you are there, you are an extension of the body of Jesus.

"While you are there under that car working, don't you think for a minute"—and then I went back up on the platform—"that there is any less nobility while you are under that car than when I am on this platform or that what you are doing there is any less important than what I am doing standing here right now."

Well, the place exploded with applause. Eight hundred men were electrified with the awareness that ministry has a value in the eyes of Jesus wherever you are every day, being what He has made you to be. And we ministers exist in our ministry to help your ministry happen. We are to maximize the possibility that wherever you are or whatever you do, the life of Jesus will have been refreshed and nourished in you.

Frankly, I deem what you do day by day far more significant in making a difference in our world than what I do. My mission is to do what I can to minister in order to help you understand how Jesus makes a difference in you. Then when you go out to places because of the gifting you have, you make a difference in the world because of the presence and life that He is working in you there. Jesus said that whenever anything terminates that—and boy, these are strong words from the Savior Himself—"I hate it."

Something else that puts religious systems in place that become counter to the glory and grace of the Lord in the Church is the practice of legalism. "The synagogue of Satan" describes the transference into the new covenant of the rigid systems of the law. It imposes them in the era of grace. We are to obey all of Scripture, but some regulations that are imposed by human tradition disallow the free flow of God's grace through the Church. Let me give two examples.

For example, some people in the Church declare, "I believe this about this, and I believe that about that. Because I can prove it with chapter and verse, I'm right. What do you think about that? And if you don't think about it the way I do you don't fit in my book; you don't fit in my system. Though you name Jesus Christ as your Savior and though you love Him with all your heart and though you believe the Bible is the Word of God and take it as seriously as I do, if you don't see my system the way I see it then you're out." That kind of dogmatism and sectarianism and the doctrinaire attitudes are destructive to the Church's life. They preempt the love of one another that should characterize the Church.

I don't believe the Lord has intended one denomination to be other than what it is. I don't think He is trying to converge everything into one massive group asserting, "We all believe the same thing." But I do believe He is saying that since we all love the same Lord, let's be big enough to come together around Him, glorify Him, love one another on those grounds, and permit each one to have distinctives on minor points of doctrine.

Another example is the tendency of people to think that servant leadership calling people to accountability is oppressive. I have seen it both ways: leaders who oppress and leaders who accept responsibility in order to see release of life.

Recently, Pastor Scott Bauer and I were dealing with a situation of oppression of a spiritual leader in a mind-control approach to supposed New Testament church life. That's legalism—the synagogue of Satan. The devil has his way of imposing on people systems that dehumanize them. But there is another place of leadership where it is not a matter of dehumanizing; it is simply calling people to accountability. And these things call for balance on a broad basis.

The replacement of religious systems that reveal glory and grace can create real problems in the Church, and it terminates the vital life of the Church.

SOLUTIONS FROM JESUS

These are the points of confrontation that Jesus made. Now, let's look at the solutions that Jesus gave.

First, *look at the Savior and listen to the Spirit.* I outlined earlier that every letter begins with a picture of Jesus in part of His trait or person that addresses the specific church's weakness. Every letter ends with, "He who has an ear, let him hear what the Spirit says to the churches." So you get this call to look at Jesus and listen to the Spirit. Keep your eyes on Jesus; keep tuned in to heaven.

Here is the second solution. In five of the letters Jesus said, "Repent." He gave direction to *repent.* Repentance means to turn, to respond to what He is saying to you and do it. It is not crying and begging for forgiveness; that is remorse. Remorse is sometimes appropriate. But Paul addressed the Corinthian church where there were some people who felt bad but didn't do anything about it: "Godly sorrow produces repentance leading to salvation . . . but the sorrow of the world produces death" (2 Cor. 7:10). The death, or termination, is not physical death in this case so much as it is the death of effectiveness.

The third solution is to *treat adversity as a friend and a refining force.* I said earlier that material success is not synonymous with blessing. Well, in two of these letters Jesus specifically addressed the issue of adversity storming in on them, but they responded grandly! They had been going through persecution, they had been going through tribulation, they had been going through every kind of assault, and it had brought them to poverty. Then He said, "You are rich." The people allowed adversity to become something that brought beauty into their lives.

The call of Jesus is to recognize when those times come and not throw in the towel or retreat whiningly to some point of private reclusiveness from reality: "I just don't understand it. I guess God is after me." Why? Because we made the earlier mistake of believing that blessing is only smooth sailing.

Loved one, sometimes tough things happen. We read that "you will have tribulation ten days" (2:10). "Ten days" references the passing of an amount of time that has no specific measure. It was a commonly used phrase in the culture of that time to describe something that seemed to go on and on and on. Ten also meant it would come to an end. But when you are going through it, it doesn't seem that it is ever going to end.

The Lord says that when that kind of adversity comes, we are to keep on keepin' on. How do we keep on keepin' on? We accept His correction with humility and spontaneity and then anticipate the victory that He has given us over the terminator. There is a certainty of victory down the line.

THE CERTAINTY OF VICTORY

The certainty of victory is wrapped up in these words: "To him who overcomes . . ." What was He saying? Jesus was saying, "I can make it possible. Overcoming is not an empty dream. There is no reason for anything of effectiveness to be terminated in My Church."

I thought of calling Jesus the Terminator Exterminator. He is the One who confronts the things that will terminate, and He can bring solutions so that there comes the fruitfulness intended by His purpose in the life of His people, His Church.

Every time Jesus said, "To him who overcomes . . . ," He was not only holding forth the promise of overcoming, the potential of overcoming, but He was also offering the inherent inner promise "I will give . . . ," and then a battery of things unfolded. He said, "I am going to give him intimacy. I am going to draw close to him. He is going to get to know Me in a way that he never has before. I am going to give him a specific identity. I am going to write his name on a white stone and give it to him." This is a specific sense of who you are in Him so that it becomes your personal possession in all of its beauty and dignity.

He also said He is going to write His name on you. And He is going to write the name of the city of His God. I have always been amused when I read that: "I will write on him the name of My God and the name of the city of My God, the New Jerusalem . . . And I will write on him My new name" (3:12).

You know what that sounds like to me? I don't know that this is what it is supposed to mean, but Jesus was saying, "I put My name on him, and I put the name of the city so that he has been appropriately addressed. No matter how confused he gets there is an address on him that says he is going to get home. He is going to find his way there." There is a promise of overcoming triumph.

He says to those who overcome that He is going to work in them the same quality of refinement that made His feet like brass. He is going to cause them to rule over the nations. He is not talking about political clout. He is talking about the authority of the living Church when it comes into its intercessory ministry.

There are implications for the millennial destiny of the Church, too, when we will rule with Christ in the future; however, that is to manifest in its time. But He calls the Church to dominion now and says that He wants us to partner and fellowship with Him now. He puts it in these words: "Look, look [behold is the word; it sounds so much more spiritual], I am standing at the door, and I am knocking. If you hear My voice [he who has an ear, let him hear], open the door and I will come in, and we are going to get together." I want to tell you, if you and I get together with Jesus at dinner, the terminator doesn't stand a chance.

Listen to Jesus: "I stand at the door and knock" (Rev. 3:20). How personal to have Jesus on the porch of your soul. He says, "I am ready to come in, but the invitation is yours to issue. I am available." If you let Him in, He will preempt the capacity of anything to terminate what you are intended to be in His purpose, and if that happens in all of us, then there are no limits on what He can do in us as a body of people. That is why He wrote to churches. The message comes individually and personally, but He wrote to groups of people. He wants us to be a people so that His fullest life can happen through us.

5

COME INTO THE ROCK

REVELATION 4:1–11

After these things I looked, and behold, a door standing open in heaven. And the first voice which I heard was like a trumpet speaking with me, saying, "Come up here, and I will show you things which must take place after this." Immediately I was in the Spirit; and behold, a throne set in heaven, and One sat on the throne. And He who sat there was like a jasper and a sardius stone in appearance; and there was a rainbow around the throne, in appearance like an emerald. Around the throne were twenty-four thrones, and on the thrones I saw twenty-four elders sitting, clothed in white robes; and they had crowns of gold on their heads. And from the throne proceeded lightnings, thunderings, and voices. Seven lamps of fire were burning before the throne, which are the seven Spirits of God. Before the throne there was a sea of glass, like crystal. And in the midst of the throne, and around the throne, were four living creatures full of eyes in front and in back. The first living creature was like a lion, the second living creature like a calf, the third living creature had a face like a man, and the fourth living creature was like a flying eagle. The four living creatures, each having six wings, were full of eyes around and within. And they do not rest day or night, saying:

"Holy, holy, holy,
Lord God Almighty,
Who was and is and is to come!"

Whenever the living creatures give glory and honor and thanks to Him who sits on the throne, who lives forever and ever, the twenty-four elders fall down before Him who sits on the throne and worship Him who lives forever and ever, and cast their crowns before the throne, saying:

"You are worthy, O Lord,
To receive glory and honor and power;
For You created all things,
And by Your will they exist and were created." (Rev. 4:1–11)

An Unusual Experience

One of the most peculiar things that has ever happened to me happened when my attention was called to this passage of Scripture (Rev. 4:1–11) in a very special moment. It happened like this.

It was a Tuesday morning twenty-seven or twenty-eight years ago. The only place we had at our church was the little chapel that is twice as big now as it was then. Our attendance at that time was sixty to seventy-five people. For some reason we were having a men's prayer meeting that morning, and about six guys were there. That was a pretty great turnout, given the time of the morning and the size of the church.

In any case, I was hardly tuned to what most people would think to be a "spiritual" wavelength. It was six o'clock in the morning, and I don't come whistling out of bed at five-thirty. In short, I was *there* but I certainly was not feeling "with it."

So you can imagine my surprise, while I knelt in prayer with anything but a mystical mind-set and definitely feeling untuned to heaven, when I sensed God "speaking" to me. My impression of His words will not make sense to you at all unless I tell you what had happened a few days earlier.

Some of us of the pastoral staff were praying in the sanctuary. At one point, I felt strongly prompted to have each person stand at a corner of the sanctuary. So, we scattered to the four corners of the room. I said, "Let's extend our hands to the middle of the room as if we are lifting up a canopy of praise to the Lord, like a tabernacle." As we began to praise the Lord, something really beautiful happened. There came an invasion of the sense of the presence of God.

I suppose for twenty or thirty minutes we were carried along on a sense of the buoyancy of the spirit of praise while we worshiped the Lord. Then our youth pastor, who was standing in the corner of the room diagonally from where I was, stepped forward as there was a lull in the praise and the singing and the worship. He said, "The Lord just impressed on me very strongly the reason that this seems so right. Each of us is standing at a corner of this sanctuary, and we are aligned with four angelic beings who are always there. We are kind of harmonizing with the heavenlies right now. Our praise is entering into another dimension at the same time."

He was not a mystical type of guy and wasn't saying that to try to impress us with some unique spirituality on his part or to suggest that we were something special. It was an observation that he felt the Lord had given him.

You know, we sing songs, "I can hear the brush of angels' wings, I see glory on each face," so it is not a concept that is strange to us. It is a biblical idea that there is a convergence of the visible and the invisible when worship is alive and real. And he had mentioned the four angels at the corners of the room.

That's about all there was to it. We praised God, and we sang a little more and worshiped. Then for all intents and purposes, I forgot about the situation.

Now, I was trying to keep awake there in that prayer meeting, and while I knelt, I was being taught: "The four angels that Paul [our youth pastor] mentioned the other night are the four living creatures of the book of Revelation, chapter 4." (Forgive me, please, but I nearly laughed out loud. Even though I now was sensitive to the presence of God impressing my heart with understanding—even though I was confident it was His Spirit teaching me—the idea struck me as more than merely peculiar.) *C'mon, sure! [I chuckled to myself.] The four living creatures of the book of Revelation, which are in closest proximity to the throne of God of any of the angelic beings. These? The ones that stimulate the praise of the universe? These? The ones crying, "Holy, holy,*

holy is the Lord of hosts," as all heaven bows before Your *throne?* (It sounded ludicrous to suggest they had come from heaven to 14344 Sherman Way in Van Nuys, California.) *They are here?! Where else would they go?* I thought, mockingly. I suddenly wanted to dismiss it all and shout, "My, Lord! There have been entire cult systems started with less material than this!!"

I didn't say any of that, but I got up from my knees. Up on the platform behind the pulpit there was a Communion table that had an open pulpit Bible on it. I went up and paged to the fourth chapter of Revelation and stood there while the men were praying. I didn't say anything to anybody about that. Believe me, I didn't tell them! I read the fourth chapter of Revelation, and I didn't have any more insight than if I had read it before that happened. I let it go. That's it. And I forgot about it.

About a week and a half went by. I want to emphasize that I had not tried to figure this out at all. I drove into the driveway of the church after I had been lecturing at the college, got out of the car, and walked toward the church building to take care of some business in my office. I got about a third of the way to the building, and all of a sudden, without premeditating or thinking about it, I saw something that I want to tell you about because it relates to this text and all the implications of this text. It relates to something that I believe is essential for you to do personally, and it relates to something that I believe the Lord is calling us to do corporately. It calls us to action.

"Have You Ever Had the Experience of . . . ?"

But before I get there, I want to ask you to walk through this passage with me and other references that have to do with

Jesus disclosing Himself and His heart toward His Church and His purpose among all of us and throughout the earth. I want you to think with me about this by my asking three questions. All of them begin, "Have you ever had the experience of . . . ?"

1. Have you ever had the experience of attempting to do something sincerely loving and kind for someone and then having him throw it back in your face?

2. Have you ever had the experience of showing every effort at helping in a situation and having the door closed in your face?

3. Have you ever had the experience of watching something you've spent years building seem to disintegrate before your eyes, but you can't do anything about it?

I want to open these three questions to your thinking because I believe they reflect the mood and the context as John received the words from Jesus at the beginning of chapter 4 of the book of Revelation. I want you to think with me about the opening words: "After these things I looked, and behold, a door standing open in heaven" (4:1).

Remember where we left off in the last chapter. The seven letters that had just been dictated to John by Jesus were to be sent to the seven churches in Asia Minor. It was Asia Minor by the boundary specifications of the ancient Roman Empire province called Asia Minor. It was not the same as the Asia Minor that we usually see as the portion of the Middle East called Turkey today, which thrusts westward and comes out a giant land mass that ends on the west coast of that portion of land at the Aegean Sea. I am not talking about Asia Minor of that size. It was a province that probably was 175 to 200 miles north and south and 150 or 200 miles across, located at the west end of what we call Asia Minor today. There would have been other congregations scattered through that area, but seven congregations were the primary points of influence. John was the one responsible for them. He was the bishop, the overseer, of the churches, and they were much on his heart.

John had given a great deal of his service and effort to shape, to serve, and to help the churches come to be what they were called to be. The Son of God Himself, the Lord of the Church, dictated to him a letter for each church. Five of the seven letters spoke of things being in serious disrepair in those churches in sizable segments of the congregation.

A faithful servant, an outstanding man of God, John could not help feeling bad about the circumstances. Things seemed to be coming unglued at those churches, but there was nothing he could do about it because he was imprisoned on Patmos. He was in prison because he had tried to serve humanity with the love of God and had been shut up for it. He had sought to do what he knew his life was about. There was no reasonable excuse for his being treated as he was.

The things that were true of John are the same things that we feel. At times we may feel as helpless as a baby and want to cry like one. The feelings were of a rejected offer of a loving action, a refused offer of gracious service, and a feeling of helplessness before a disappointment.

Direction from the Lord

These feelings summarize pretty well where Anna and I were recently. A confluence of things happened to us. I got up one morning feeling the weight of all those things. As I went to my place of devotions, I felt a touch from the Lord and a whisper in my ear: *Come into the Rock. Come into the Rock.* I understood immediately what it meant. In fact, I jotted the words in my journal, *Come into the Rock,* because I knew the Lord was saying three things to me.

1. A Sure Defense

First, *the Lord was calling me to find a sure defense.* You know, if we don't find our defense in the Lord during tough times, we're going to go about trying to defend ourselves. Then we create more problems than the problems we started defending against. When people do things to us, misunderstand us, or reject us, a natural reaction is to protest, "Now wait just a minute!" And we tell people, "I was trying to do so and so and so and so," and we start building a defense for ourselves. The problem is that we are not really good at it. We think we are, but inevitably, our efforts drive a wedge deeper one way or the other. One group of people may side with us, but then the individuals against whom we are defending ourselves may deepen their case and the problem intensifies. Self-defensiveness doesn't work.

The Bible calls us to let the Lord be our defender. David learned that truth a long, long time ago. Time and again in the Psalms he declared, "Lord, You are my shield." We sing the old hymn, "We rest in Thee our Shield and our Defender," or we sing, "A mighty fortress is our God." And while we sing, we still too readily leap to our own defense when some of the things like those I recited take place. The Lord was saying to me, "Son, you need to come into the Rock because that is the only place you've got a sure defense."

2. REST FROM MY PRESENT TENSE

There is a second thing the Lord was saying to me: *the Rock is the only place I can find rest from my present tense.* That is obviously a play on words, considering the tension and the pressure that were on me.

The Bible calls us to keep on being filled with the Spirit. Ephesians 5 explains that we should keep being filled with the Spirit so that we can discern the mind of the Lord, see the will of God released in our lives, and redeem the time because "the days are evil" (Eph. 5:16).

The Greek noun that was translated "evil" does not refer to something that is sinister or suspect, as we think of evil in its most vicious forms. But it is evil in the sense of accumulating force sufficient to feel its pressure. It is like a siege being laid to a city.

When pressure comes upon my precious wife, the tension across her back takes a horrible, physical toll on her body. It is not a matter of massaging it, and the tension will go away. It becomes a burden like a yoke strapped on her back.

We were both feeling something like that at the time when the Lord said, "Come into the Rock." He was saying to come there because we were going to burn out if we tried to carry the load ourselves. The present tensions that we faced needed to be taken somewhere and left there. An old song has the line: "Take your burden to the Lord and leave it there." We were to cast our burden upon the Lord, and He would sustain us. We were to come into the Rock to rest our present tense.

3. A BATTLE STANCE

The third thing I understood from the Lord was that *I was to take a battle stance.* But I had to do the other things first. If I took a battle stance before I made the Lord my defense, I would start battling in a self-defensive way. And if I took a battle stance before I rested my case in His hands and in His power, I would try to function in my own energy, and I would end up focusing on the people or the circumstance that I perceived to be the problem instead of the real source of the things that assail us. The real source is not that we're wrestling against flesh and blood and human circumstance; we are wrestling against dark powers. And once we come into the place of the Rock, saying, "He's my Rock, He's my Fortress" then we can proclaim, "He's my Deliverer."

Those words we sing so often, right out of Psalm 18, call us to take the battle stance in the Rock with dependence upon the power of the Lord to become our resource. Those things were spoken to me, and I reached an understanding of them almost immediately before I was to begin my study in the preparation of this chapter. I turned here where the Lord said to John, "Come up here, and I will show you . . ." (Rev. 4:1).

I don't think that I would have seen the parallel between these words to John and their practical application to John if it weren't for what I had been facing. Don't think I am imposing something on the text that is merely the basis of a subjective feeling. We often suppose that John received the Revelation and just sat down with his papyri and stylus and ripped it off while the words were coming. Because we can read this book in about an hour, we figure he must have written it in a couple of hours while it was happening.

A DOOR INTO GOD'S PRESENCE

Revelation is a sequence of visions given to John. He did not give us the chronology in which the visions came, but there is no reason to think that they happened in a matter of hours or two or three days. There is no reason to think that they took a long time, either. But there is every reason to believe that there was a hiatus between the visions.

The text opens, "After these things." There has been a first part, and now we are coming to something else. And in between I want to suggest a reasonable proposition. John had dictated to him the letters that described the things concerning areas of his responsibility, the churches that he oversaw. Then he was to send the letters by the Roman mail system in the name of Jesus.

The letters dealt with problems in places where he had taught the people to do better, and he was prevented from going to them in person to offer assistance.

More than likely, John's emotions would have been very much like yours or mine in similar circumstances. You've done everything you can. You've tried to love, to serve, to help. And then what you've given yourself to build starts coming apart and you can't do anything about it. You feel as helpless as a baby.

Then the Lord Jesus appeared to him and spoke. When He

spoke, there was a trumpet sound, and the words were, "Come up here." John had written, "I looked, and behold [I want to come back to that word—it occurs twice], a door standing open in heaven" (4:1).

John was called to step into a dimension beyond human perception. That is what this is about. "Look, there is a door open." When we are in tight circumstances, tension and pressure, difficulty and pain, we tend to look for a door out. John had an open door.

However, we are going to discover that it was a door in, not a door out. It was a door into the presence of God. It was a door into the throne room of heaven where things were different from John's circumstances. The promise of His presence would make that difference as it eventually distilled into John's circumstances. There is a door *in* that opens up before all of us.

John was going to be shown the conflict of the ages between the world spirit and the Spirit of God. He was going to be shown the judgment of the earth and all the horrible implications that ultimately will come at the end of time. He was going to be shown the warfare against evil as the Church and the Beast will be in a spiritual wrestling match, and he was going to be shown the triumph of Christ and His own. In other words, he was brought to a vantage point on the future, and he could see that beyond the present circumstances were things of the triumph of God. The open door was a call to see beyond the moment.

Several years ago I and my friend Don Moen, who has written many of the songs we know and sing, were working together on a musical that was distributed quite widely entitled *God with*

Us. As we were working on that, he told me the story behind his song "God Will Make a Way." As a matter of fact, we incorporated it into the narrative of the musical because it was such a beautiful story. It was too good to pass up. But it was not a good thing that happened to spawn the song.

Don received a phone call. It was one of those shocking phone calls when tragedy is announced and you recoil from the impact of what you hear. It wasn't about his wife, Laura, or any of their children, but it was about close family members. There had been a horrible traffic accident, and members of the family were snatched into eternity. Don very quickly made arrangements to fly to the family site. While he was traveling, he was so stirred up in his grief that he was trying to think about what he would say to the remaining family members. Don said, "Jack, I was looking out the plane window, traveling there at thirty-some thousand feet, and wanting so much a word I could give them. I didn't compose this song by sitting down and thinking it up. It just rose in me and I started singing." What became a word for them became a word for others: "God will make a way when there seems to be no way. He works in ways we cannot see, He will make a way for me." The Lord understands, and He is there.

God will make a way. There is a door open. But take the door that enters in. Don't take the door that goes out. Someone reading these words right now is ready to take a door out of a marriage, a door out of some responsibility that you are sick and tired of, or a door away from a job. "I'm getting out of here. This is the pits!" Sound familiar? God will make a way; there is a door into His presence.

A Voice Like a Trumpet

To get attention, there was a trumpet call. John said the voice he heard was like a trumpet speaking. When we read the whole context and go back to chapter 1, the first time John heard Jesus personally, he said it was a voice like a trumpet, saying, "I am the Alpha and the Omega." Jesus was calling him. And when the words came to him, "Come up here, and I will show you things which must take place after this," they were not spoken softly. A voice like a trumpet said, "COME UP HERE, AND I WILL SHOW YOU THINGS WHICH MUST TAKE PLACE AFTER THIS."

Since John and Jesus had such a close relationship, why would Jesus trumpet words to him? I don't know the answer, but I have some ideas.

I'm likely not to hear Him unless it comes like a trumpet call. And you are probably the same way. When we are about to come to our own defense, try to work something out our own way, or throw in the towel, the Lord calls and says, "DON'T DO THAT! COME UP HERE!" Come into the Rock. Come up here.

Thinking of the Lord's call sounding like a trumpet reminds me of the way that Jewish people use the trumpet today. In tens of thousands of synagogues around the planet the shofar sounds to announce the new year, the beginning of a new time.

In ancient Israel, the trumpet sounded on other occasions. (You can read details in the book of Numbers.) The trumpet sounded for the people to gather for assembly. After they had packed up and were in the wilderness, the trumpet sounded to announce, "Everybody, forward march." Then there was the trumpet call to battle.

The Lord calls for a readiness and a responsiveness to His words: "Come up here." He sounds a voice like a trumpet call to us and then offers an invitation to insight. The Son of God said, "Come up here, *and I will show you things*." I like that!

We need to have many things shown to us, and they are usually things that we don't think we need to be shown. We think we have already figured them out.

BEHOLD!

Earlier, I said that I wanted to talk about the word *behold*. In forty-two years of ministering the Word of God publicly and all the study I have done in the Greek New Testament, I had never stopped before to study the word *behold*. It occurs twice in this text, and I got to thinking about it because everybody knows what *behold* means—"look" or "here is something to see."

The word *behold* occurs in the form of two different Greek words that are directly cognate. They are not that much different, but the form expresses a different mood in its usage. Of 204 times in the New Testament, 24 times it is an indication of surprise. It is almost the equivalent of "Wow!" A few times it is, "Wow, look, behold!" But 180 times it carries the idea of calling to attention but in a distinct way. These two usages in Revelation reflect the latter meaning.

The word in the Greek language is *edeu*. It is a direct cognitive verb that is important to understanding what is being said in this invitation to insight. *Edeu* is cognate to the verb *idon*. *Idon* is a verb that is one of two words in the Greek language for "to see." The most common one is *blepo,* and that is the one you would use to describe seeing as in, "I see that shrubbery in the yard. I see that piano in the living room. I see that fellow on television wearing a blue suit." We see and make observations. That is "see"—*blepo*. *Idon* is very much different. *Idon* has to do not with saying, "I see," but with saying, "Oh, I see." We perceive; we understand. This invitation of Jesus is a call to that.

John was not saying, "Well, I was there, and all of a sudden there was this voice. A door was opened and then I looked and I saw." No. He was saying, "I was there, and all of a sudden . . . '*Oh, now I see!*'" He used "behold" as an injunction to us. He wanted us to see it too. This is the whole message—an invitation to insight.

John described the first thing that he saw: "a throne set in heaven" (4:2). The word *set* conveys the concept of fixedness, immovability, unshakability. It is as though John might say, if you or I had been there and were hearing his account at the instant of his amazement, "I answered the trumpet call and the invitation. And then—among all the things that I can't control and the things that I wish were different from the way they are, I looked, I stepped inside the door, and—praise the Lord God Almighty!— I saw His immovable throne . . . His unshakable kingdom!"

This glorious revelation points to where the solidity of our lives and the security of all issues of our lives are found. As John saw the throne of God, there is something that parallels the vision of Daniel in the Old Testament. Daniel said that he saw the throne of God, and from that throne there was a disposition being made of divine authority, which eventually dashed to destruction everything that opposed God's purposes with His own. It brought about the fulfillment and completion of all that He intended for those who open themselves to Him. That was what John was seeing: "I saw a throne, and it was set. Unshakable."

The psalmist declared, "Forever, O LORD, Your word is settled in heaven" (Ps. 119:89). Not only the Scriptures are intended here. God is King, and His word cannot be altered—what He declares will be realized. That brings us to the significance of what else John saw when he looked at the throne.

The next thing that he saw was a radiance around the throne: "there was a rainbow" (4:3). There is only one logical reason for the Lord to reveal Himself in that way and to have it put by the Spirit of God in the Scriptures for us. A rainbow means one thing in the Scriptures. Scientifically, a rainbow is the spectrum of light that flashes out after the beam of white light is broken up into its manifold components. The Lord is showing us the radiance of His person, which is spread out in a way that we can see all the component splendors of His promise toward us. The first time that promise was ever spoken to mankind, a rainbow appeared to guarantee that what happened in the past in its destructiveness would not dictate what the future is going to be.

You know the story of Noah. There remains the mud from the flood that covered the earth as well as the horror of the memory of the condition of the world prior to it. Noah stepped out onto the face of an earth with a new possibility, and God showed a rainbow and said, "What has happened in the past has nothing to do with what the shape of the future is going to be."

When we come to the Lord's throne, He wants us to see not just the glory of His person, but also the splendor of His promise given to us. Hallelujah! It breaks out in so many shapes, sizes, and colors that there are a shape and a size and a color for what-ever we need today.

UNCEASING WORSHIP

So how do you access all this? John saw unceasing worship. The cherubim, those four living creatures around the throne, bowed in ceaseless worship. I mentioned earlier those four living crea-tures, and I told you it was a peculiar story because of what the Lord said to me. Without any premeditation, forethought, or attempts to compute the meaning, suddenly, it was there. The easiest way for me to describe it is this:

The Lord's word is settled forever in heaven, and His throne is unshakable and immovable. The glory of His kingdom power is disposed toward us. Promise shines from that throne, and an open door gives us access to His presence. He sent a trumpet call and extended an invitation to us to gain insight, which comes when we see that it is right to come into His presence rather than to exit somewhere else.

Anytime that you and I commit ourselves to the kind of wor-ship that occurs around the throne, we begin to come into align-ment with His throne. As we draw near to God, the Bible says that He draws near to us. There is space for as many people as will choose to come. Because we are into the realm of eternity, there is room for all. And the angelic beings are around because we have drawn close to His throne.

Recognize that this is personal. As He called to John, the Lord calls to you, "Come up here." The Lord said to me, "Come into the Rock."

Be willing to take to Him whatever concerns you. Is it a family matter? Is it a business issue? Is it something that has to do with factors in your life that make you feel as helpless as a baby? Enter in.

Understand that there is a word to us. I would like to take every reader by the hand and say in the name of Jesus, "Come here." Here's what I would be talking about. I would not preach a whole message from the timeless Word of God to make one point about one time. But I believe the Spirit of God has called us to a new time, and it impacts us all. We say, "Lord, we know where the action is. Everything that happens in this world to make a difference happens because of the glory and power and promise of Jesus' throne. And we want to be committed freshly to worship there."

Would you personally make that commitment with regard to yourself? With regard to the matters of your life?

We need to respond to this revelation of Jesus, who calls us with a voice like a trumpet, who invites us to insight, who comes to usher us into the Father's presence. All of His majesty is beaming forth promise from the throne, and He says, "Come worship here. That is the way you find your sure defense, you rest your present tense, you take your battle stance, and you move into the future."

6

UNDERSTANDING THE E BOOK

And I saw in the right hand of Him who sat on the throne a scroll written inside and on the back, sealed with seven seals. Then I saw a strong angel proclaiming with a loud voice, "Who is worthy to open the scroll and to loose its seals?" And no one in heaven or on the earth or under the earth was able to open the scroll, or to look at it. So I wept much, because no one was found worthy to open and read the scroll, or to look at it. But one of the elders said to me, "Do not weep. Behold, the Lion of the tribe of Judah, the Root of David, has prevailed to open the scroll and to loose its seven seals." And I looked, and behold, in the midst of the throne and of the four living creatures, and in the midst of the elders, stood a Lamb as though it had been slain, having seven horns and seven eyes, which are the seven Spirits of God sent out into all the earth. Then He came and took the scroll out of the right hand of Him who sat on the throne. Now when He had taken the scroll, the four living creatures and the twenty-four elders fell down before the Lamb, each having a harp, and golden bowls full of incense, which are the prayers of the saints. (Rev. 5:1–8)

These bowls full of incense are the prayers of the saints. This point is important because there is a good deal of superstition about incense and worship of or praise to God. Worship and praise and prayer are fragrances before the throne of God when they come from hearts that are open to Him.

BIBLICAL SAINTS

You may be unfamiliar with the biblical use of the word *saints*. There is a difference between the biblical usage and the traditional church usage of the word.

In traditional use, the word *saints* refers to a relatively small group of people. Approximately 1,400 people throughout two thousand years have been designated by the traditional church as being saints. This designation notes noble deeds of the person, and it is a worthy recognition. I don't have any hesitation about saying that. However, I think it is unfortunate that the word is used that way because it suggests that the word *saints* in the Bible refers to an exclusive few.

In the Bible, the word *saints* refers to all of us who have put our trust in Jesus Christ as Savior. But we don't designate ourselves. No human being has the right to designate a saint. We can say that someone is a great person and does outstanding things, but God is the only One who has the right to say that someone is holy in His sight. He says that of you and me when we put our trust in Jesus, whether or not we have noble or outstanding or remarkable achievements. In fact, He does it in spite of our achievements. And He designates that we are saints. So, if you put your trust in Jesus, verse 8 is talking about your prayers. In heaven, your prayers smell good!

And they sang a new song, saying:

"You are worthy to take the scroll,
And to open its seals;
For You were slain,
And have redeemed us to God by Your blood
Out of every tribe and tongue and people and nation,
And have made us kings and priests to our God;
And we shall reign on the earth."

Then I looked, and I heard the voice of many angels around the throne, the living creatures, and the elders; and the number of them was ten thousand times ten thousand, and thousands of thousands, saying with a loud voice:

"Worthy is the Lamb who was slain
To receive power and riches and wisdom,
And strength and honor and glory and blessing!"

And every creature which is in heaven and on the earth and under the earth and such as are in the sea, and all that are in them, I heard saying:

"Blessing and honor and glory and power
Be to Him who sits on the throne,
And to the Lamb, forever and ever!"

Then the four living creatures said, "Amen!" And the twenty-four elders fell down and worshiped Him who lives forever and ever. (Rev. 5:9–14)

THE ULTIMATE SCROLL

The title of this chapter is "Understanding the E Book" ("E" or "End," the End Book). The E Book is not the last book in the Bible. It is a book within the book. It is described eight times in nine verses and called the scroll. And in a very real sense it is the ultimate scroll.

Let me quickly explain a couple of things about scrolls. The book of Revelation refers to other scrolls. There is reference to the book of Revelation itself as a book or a scroll. *Biblion* is the Greek word translated "scroll." It may help to know about earlier practices of writing and publishing. Biblical writing was done on a sheet of papyrus about eight inches wide and ten inches long. (Most of our paper today is eight and a half by eleven inches.) There were two columns on it, each about three inches wide, written in the language of the times, in this case, the Greek language.

When a document was longer than one sheet, the sheets were attached to one another. Then to store them or to take them from place to place, they were rolled or scrolled up. That is what is being described. For example, the scroll of the book of Revelation is approximately fifteen feet long. This figure comes from the actual measure of scrolls that have survived from that time. The gospel of John is almost twenty-five feet long. The book of Philemon, a very small, one-chapter book, is on one page. So the lengths varied.

Some scrolls were used as books, but a distinct kind of scroll was sealed in the same way that this one was sealed. A scroll with those kinds of seals was probably a will.

In Roman times—and Revelation was written in Roman times—when a person prepared his will, seven witnesses attested to the will, and each one sealed it. Wax was poured on the place where it was sealed, and they signed the place where they had sealed or attested to the will. When the person died and the will was to be executed, the seals could be broken only by each witness or a legal representative of each witness, who was present for the unsealing of the scroll and its reading. This is one of those scrolls.

I call this the E Book for several reasons. The foremost reason is that this book within the book of Revelation, which begins its description here in chapter 5 and begins to be unsealed in chapter 6, is easily confused because we get caught up in a series of sevens that follow through the next ten chapters of Revelation. There are seven seals, seven trumpets, and seven bowls. If you are familiar with the book of Revelation, you know something of their significance. I will say more about the convergence of these three sevens later in the book.

This scroll unfolds the whole of everything that happens in chapters 5 through 18 of the book of Revelation. Then what happens in the final four chapters (chaps. 19–22) has to do with the result of the unscrolling of the scroll.

This scroll is the centerpiece of the book of Revelation. Let that be fixed in your mind. I am persuaded that unless we understand the E Book, we won't understand what is really in motion in Revelation—other than that there is a whole lot of turmoil, followed by a nice ending to the story.

There are reasons behind the turmoil, a reason for it, and a reason that it has to happen before we come to the nice ending. It all has to do with understanding the E Book and what it was in the first place. It is a will. There was something behind that will. And we capture a sense of whose will it is when we see who is holding it at the beginning of chapter 5.

Successive sets of action are administered by the hand of Jesus, the Lamb of God as a result of what takes place in chapter 5. Chapter 5 continues chapter 4. We have already learned about John's being called up into the throne room of heaven. As he stepped through the door that was opened before him, he was overwhelmed by the awesome scene of worship. At the very end of chapter 4 the words were those of worship by the cherubim and the elders: "You are worthy, O Lord." They spoke of the One who has created all things and of His will. See that? "By Your will they exist and were created" (4:11). Capture that statement about the will of God and His creation of all things for heavenly design and benevolent purposes.

Continuing as though there was not a chapter division, John said, "And I saw in the right hand of the One they were worshiping on the throne a scroll written on the front and back sides. There were seven seals upon the scroll, and an angel proclaimed, 'Who can open the scroll?'"

What Does the Scroll Contain?

I want to discuss the scroll by answering some questions. The first question is, What does the scroll contain?

This passage of Scripture is a continuation of the subject of the will of God. Wills were sealed. The will of God was seen, then inscribed, in a sense, in His hand. It is a depiction of His will. We could say that the will of God is something in His mind or His heart, and that is true. It is revealed in very real ways in the Scriptures, and we see something of His will there.

This passage has to do with a specific issue: the will of God regarding this planet. Everything that takes place in the book of Revelation focuses on what the Lord is doing on this planet and what He is doing with mankind. It has to do with what He originally wanted to be experienced by mankind, what came to be experienced by mankind, and what God is doing to release what He originally intended for mankind.

A Place for Mankind

To understand the E Book, we really need to be reminded of how the whole book of Scripture begins. The Bible begins with God creating this earth for mankind to dwell on. He specifically describes what He wants mankind to know on this earth. Do not make any mistake: when we talk about mankind in the light of the Scriptures, we have a vastly different perspective from that of the philosophical system prevalent in the world.

I have never felt obligated to argue with people over the issues of evolution because it is really not so much a scientific proposition as it is an issue of faith—a matter of what you choose to believe. Belief in evolution is actually no more scientific than belief in Scripture. Indeed, recent opinions of astronomers confirm the biblical record of creation's beginnings, but that isn't my point. My point is that God planned the earth as a place for mankind. Isaiah 45:18 describes the full scenario—(1) how He first *created* our world (from the Hebrew *bara,* meaning "to beget without preexisting material"—Gen. 1:1, 31); (2) how He *formed and made* the world (from the Hebrew *yahtzar/gahsah*) in a short-term "reconditioning" program following the ruin of the earth's original order through some cosmic, destructive event that brought chaos to creation; and (3) how, having renewed our planet as a beautiful dwelling place in a distinct and separate act of creation, God created humankind (Gen. 1:27).

To assert that humans are *not* the result of evolution is not to rule out the possibility that the earth is very, very old—perhaps as much as five billion to fifteen billion years old, as some scientists suggest. But humankind and our story are relatively recent and brief by comparison. We are not the product of millions of years of natural selection but the result of divine selection—specially created beings with high destiny and eternal significance. God made us to experience the joys of fruitfulness in life, the multiplying of family and its pleasures, a culture and atmosphere untainted by sin's destructiveness, and the prospect of dominion being given to us (Gen. 1:28).

The word *dominion* is key here. Human dominion on earth meant that God was giving mankind the responsibility and the untainted capacity to develop and govern a planet—one to be cultivated in all its potential *without* the inhibiting presence of sickness, death, or evil. That was what God willed for humans when He created us and when He bestowed on us the awesome possibilities of rule or dominion.

To explore all the possibilities of that truth staggers the imagination, given the unlimited capacities originally given to us. My personal conviction is that every discovery or technological invention that we know today would have been developed *sooner* except for the fall of mankind. And they would have come with all of the benefit and none of the potential evil introduced by the curse of sin. For example, learning to harness the power of the atom would have brought only blessing, without introducing a sword of Damocles over our heads, ever threatening our destruction. All in all, without sin, without human power lust, without the self-centeredness of fallen flesh that now attempts dominion, our world would have been a much different place.

THE FALL

God had a better plan for earth—for mankind—only it hasn't happened. And it hasn't happened because of the Fall. That is the term we use for man's stepping outside obedience to and alignment with the will and purpose of God. And worse, in doing that, man submitted himself to the rule of the serpent or the dragon—the symbolic terms for Satan, a very real, sinister being who opposes God and hates everything that is of God. As this resistance to the purpose of God has manifested through mankind, it has earned for earth a *curse*.

The first pages within the E Book help us to understand a number of things. It contains first and foremost a plan that God intended for man but a plan that has been sadly defiled. Written on the inside and the back side were things that describe a curse. You may ask, "How do you know that, Pastor Jack? Why do you think a curse is written there?" The answer is found in a companion prophecy in the Old Testament.

A parallel to John's vision, as he has stepped into the throne room of heaven and seen these many things, is in the book of Zechariah. Nearly six hundred years earlier, Zechariah had looked upon a similar scene, seeing the throne room of heaven in the same *sense* but not at the same *juncture* of cosmic history. Zechariah saw the scroll, and he described what was on it:

> Then I turned and raised my eyes, and saw there a flying scroll. And he [a divine messenger] said to me, "What do you see?" So I answered, "I see a flying scroll . . ." Then he said to me, "This is the curse that goes out over the face of the whole earth: 'Every thief shall be expelled,' according to this side of the scroll; and, 'Every perjurer shall be expelled,' according to that side of it."
>
> "I will send out the curse," says the LORD of hosts;
> "It shall enter the house of the thief
> And the house of the one who swears falsely by My name."
> (Zech. 5:1–4)

When Zechariah asked the Lord, "What is the scroll?" he was told that the writing was a curse that would achieve two things: expel the thief and expel the perjurer—the liar.

I don't know if that rings a bell in your mind, but it sounds remarkably like Jesus' words describing the master thief, the master liar—Satan, who seeks to ruin all things on earth.

THE REDEEMER'S PLAN

Jesus described Satan's enterprise this way: "The thief does not come except to steal, and to kill, and to destroy." Then the Savior described His own plan: "I have come that they may have life, and that they may have it more abundantly" (John 10:10). Lay hold of this—the Redeemer's plan is to overthrow the deceiver's plan—because our understanding the implications of the book of Revelation's future message depends on grasping this.

God has ultimately ordained the recovery on this earth of what has been lost in the past, by reason of human failure or Satan's furies. It is to begin now in the lives of people who enter into the will of God through Jesus Christ. He wants for people to come to know, as it were, the personal scrolls of their lives beginning to be unsealed, for the Savior to come and open up what they were intended to be and what God wanted them to know. They don't have to wait until heaven someday to know much of the good God has for them. He wants to begin unfolding His will right now. That was what Jesus meant when He said He came to bring life more abundantly now. He wasn't only pointing to a someday in the sweet by-and-by. There is meant to be present-moment manifestations of the rule of the Lamb of God as He overthrows the work of the thief, stealing from people; the Law of God overthrows the work of the liar who would like to perpetuate confusion in the human mind.

Are you ready for a present participation in the implications of Revelation? Let's get in now!

RELEASE THROUGH JUDGMENT

The scroll is also intended to be opened to put an end to the serpent's rule on the earth. As "title deed" to the earth, it holds a promise, but human sin and satanic evil have fouled and brought a curse instead. Revelation opens our eyes to the opening of the scroll, and this opening is scheduled to bring a release from the curse via judgment that will expel the liar-thief. It is at this point that we discover the visual depictions and this unfolding of judgment that will drive out the curse.

The book of Revelation is built on a series of sevens—seven seals, seven trumpets, and seven bowls. They unfold in a unique and special way. These all intertwine and overlap in occurrence but must be read successively for the obvious reason that we can't read a jumble of words that intersect one another all at once. I will elaborate on these timing issues of the book of Revelation later. But for now, see how the scroll's seals are broken and a horrendous release of judgment ensues.

The purpose of the judgment is not retaliatory. In other words, God is not saying, "I have had it up to *here* with earth and mankind." He is not sidling up to humanity and saying, "I'm bigger than you are, and payday has come." God is not *retaliatory;* but these judgments are *retributive.* Let me describe the difference.

Retaliation occurs when someone says, "I am going to get even." Retribution occurs when something has taken place and a consequence of that action follows—and nothing can change it. It is a natural by-product of a violation of essential order.

There is a better way the Lord meant life to be. That is why He gave the laws that He has given. Some people believe that the laws of God are random and arbitrary, as though God demands, "I want you to do it this way because I am in charge." Rather, the Lord is saying, "I have created things to work in a way that will be good for you. Here are the guidelines so that you don't ruin the equipment and mess everything up."

As human beings in a fallen state, we figure, "Well, I'll tamper with the law a little bit and see what happens." Then things blow up in our faces when we violate the laws of God. That is retribution, but at a limited level. Retribution that comes upon the whole earth results from mankind getting out of sync with all that God has intended.

This release of judgment is not from God's throwing a tantrum in heaven and the vibrations rattling our cages on earth. It is the by-product of a self-invoked judgment. In other words, God is not in heaven passing out curses; rather He is saying, "I want to see the back of the curse broken." Thus He sets about driving out the systems and the spirit that administer the curse— the world, the thief, and the liar. The scales of cosmic justice will be balanced, and the earth must reap that horrible harvest it has sown unto itself.

FINALIZING THE IMPACT OF THE CURSE

The scroll's opening finalizes the impact of the curse that sin has brought. We have discussed this—the liar and the thief is driven out, and we see the thief's reign broken.

I want to say this very clearly so that you don't miss it. This is not good only for *that Day.* The Lamb begins to administer my life, not just His final administration of earth's details, when I say, "Jesus, be my Lord. I ask You to be the Executor of the Father's will in my life." That is what I am saying when I say I want the will of God in my life. Jesus died so that the will could be released and realized. And as soon as I open up to it, it begins to happen in me. So the breaking of the rule of the thief and the liar is not something for a distant day. It is a preliminary experience at a personal level of what we see here for earth and mankind at a panoramic level at a future time.

WHO SEALED THE SCROLL?

Our second question is, Who sealed the scroll? Father God. He is the One who holds it in His hand. And it is in His hand for the following reasons.

OUR SOVEREIGN GOD

It is in His hand because it demonstrates that He is the ultimate controller of earth's destiny. Father God is the One who is sovereign. No matter what may go on in this world, God didn't make up all the things that are going to foul up life on earth today.

Not long ago, a well-known athlete had surgery for cancer. Many people said, "Well, I just don't understand why God allows these things to happen." *These things* have nothing to do with things God intended. You may protest, "Well, if He is the controller of earth's destiny . . ." Wait! I said, "earth's *destiny*," not everything that happens on this planet because of the free will of human beings. Our choices—whether mistreating the body, mistreating one another, or being misaligned with the will of God—all reap their own harvest.

Still, in this passage of Scripture there is an eloquent statement that says above and beyond it all, God has never let go of the scroll. Someone reading these words right now is involved in a situation that makes it seem that hell is having its ultimate heyday. And it looks completely out of control because of the way a person is acting or the way circumstances are coming down. I want to tell you that beyond whatever is going on, there is One who has the final word and who still has His hand available to come into your situation, dear one.

We sing about it oftentimes—and don't you ever forget it. God didn't cause all the things that happen in this world, but He hasn't let go of this world yet, no, sir! And He is not going to!

Never make the mistake of blaming God for all the things that happen. He is not controlling every issue, but He has the ultimate and final control of all destiny. And you can invite His control by admitting, "This situation is out of control. But in the name of Jesus Christ of Nazareth, I pray, Father God, let Your kingdom come, Your will be done here on earth as it is in heaven." If you do, He will step in—hallelujah!

THE CURSE RESTRAINED

Also, realize this: Because the scroll is in His hand the curse's worst is restrained. This horror breaking out in the book of Revelation could have happened a long time ago. Why hasn't it? Because of the restraining hand of God. Every one of us would have far more devastating experiences except for the restraining hand of God. Every one of us would be dead meat on a hook and in the freezer under the grip of the devil if he had full control. And the same goes for our world. But the restraining, prevenient mercies of the hand of God have kept things at some degree of present equilibrium, and He hasn't yet released the final things that will execute the implications of the curse in order to drain the cup and then to start fresh. Thank God, right now He is restraining much that would otherwise occur.

GOD'S WILL REINSTATED

Finally, the scroll is in His hand because He wants to see His will reinstated. As I have already said, that is a personal issue, and you don't need to wait until the end of time for that to happen.

If you have never opened your heart to the love and the will of God, the invitation is extended to you. You can beat or batter your way through life or go along feeling smug about what is apparent, but temporary, success. But I will tell you, dear one, on your own terms you're heading for a dismal encounter with your own limitations.

Start a relationship with God. He wants to work His will in your life now. He will ultimately work His will anyway. The difference is that you can voluntarily submit to it now or, someday, find that you have cast yourself on the opposite side of it. When His will, being superimposed now without waiting on humanity, forces the flushing out of everything else with this horrendous sequence of judgments that have been sown by mankind, you remain vulnerable to that rather than realizing what would have been His will now and forever.

Jesus was made to be a curse for us (Gal. 3:13). He who knew no sin was made to be sin for us. He bore the impact of the curse that you need not. But if you choose not to receive what He has done for you and allow Him to be the One who, as your Savior, bears the curse, the curse retributively comes back upon your head.

WHY IS THERE CONCERN LEST THE SCROLL REMAIN SEALED?

Why is there concern in this text lest the scroll remain sealed? That is the third question. The concern is obvious when we read, "No one in heaven or on the earth or under the earth was able to open the scroll, or to look at it. So I wept much" (5:3–4).

As you read that, did it occur to you that John knew what was in the scroll? He knew of its implications, or there would be no reason for his weeping.

He wept *much*. He felt passionately about the matter because John understood the things we have talked about here. He understood the issues and the release of God's benevolent will toward mankind—the casting out of the thief and the liar as well as the reconciliation of all things unto God and His purposes being revealed at a human level. His concern was not just panoramic, "Oh, I wish the world was a better place!"

John had been in ministry for sixty years. He understood and loved people. I will tell you, if anything happens in your heart when you pastor or serve like a shepherd as John was a shepherd to the flock of God, you come to identify with human pain, and you care a lot. Each case is a problem with a human face, and you walk with people through the hell of some human experiences. Some of those things you experience yourself, and you realize that Jesus opened up a door of possibility for such things to be overthrown and for a change, a transformation, to occur by grace and salvation's deliverance.

THE PATHOS OF HEAVEN

John wept because he knew that if the scroll could be unsealed, things would be different. Probably the best way to describe this pathos that heaven feels—and please note it is more than the apostle John's—is that he was identifying with what we see in the person of Jesus. One of the best-known verses in the Bible is the shortest verse: "Jesus wept" (John 11:35).

Let me briefly describe the situation. Within a few months Jesus' crucifixion would take place, but no one knew about that yet. Jesus knew what He was there for—to accomplish human redemption—and He knew as He approached the tomb of Lazarus what He was going to do. He was going to resurrect Lazarus from the dead, and yet as Jesus approached the tomb, the Bible says that He groaned deeply within Himself and He wept. Why?

The reason is twofold. First, the heart of Jesus, the incarnate Son of God, felt compassion and grief with the whole human dilemma. "Yes, I am going to raise Lazarus, and this will become an important sign that I am the Messiah." He knew that—but beyond that, there are so many who die and there are so many tears and there is so much pain when loved ones die.

Second, the Son of God wept because of the knowledge within Him that there will be hosts over the course of human history who will deny the offer of grace that will superimpose the redemptive, releasing, resurrecting life of the love of God and will suffer not only a temporal death but also an eternal one.

John wept much because until that scroll is unsealed, hell will have its way. Until that scroll is unsealed, heaven's purposes will not be realized.

Dear one, in a very real sense you and I, when we enter into strong intercession for people we know and care about and find ourselves weeping, are partnering with Jesus. We are imploring that the power of God come and with His love warm the hearts of those who resist His way. We can't make the choice for them, and God can't make the choice for them. But we can weep and labor in prayer and pray that there will come the breaking of the sealed circumstance that holds only curse for them unless they accept the love and grace of God.

This is more than a theological idea. This is a personal dilemma of pain. That was why John was concerned, lest the scroll remain sealed.

WHAT DO WE LEARN WITH THE LAMB'S ARRIVAL?

Question number four: What do we learn with the Lamb's arrival? *We understand that He has the right to open the scroll:* "Look, look, the Lion of the tribe of Judah. Here is One to open the scroll." The significance of His being able to take the scroll says something about His distinction from everybody else. We read in the text, "No one in heaven or on the earth or under the earth" (5:3). In other words, no angelic presence in heaven can open the scroll. No human being on earth can open the scroll. No demon of hell is able to open the scroll.

You might think, *Why doesn't God Himself open the scroll?* Because it has to do with the administration of earth's affairs. Genesis 1 and Psalm 115 make plain that dominion was given to man; God has left to mankind the affairs of earth. *Why doesn't God do something?* He always will when He is invited. But what takes place on this planet He has decreed will take place only when human beings will it to be so. And we can will the will of God, will our own wills, or cooperate with Satan's will.

God holds what is His will for earth. It can be released only if there can be found a worthy human being, which is why He became one. The Word became flesh so that we could understand God and so that there would be One of this human race who was not tainted by sin or the curse. This One would be able to survive bearing the weight of the burden of that curse for the whole race on Himself and rise again, stand victorious, and say, "Now, in behalf of this race that is under the curse, I step inside heaven's doors and receive from the Father the scroll." He is worthy to take it. He has enough clout; He has the right. The word *worthy* has to do with His having met every required qualification through His righteousness by the power of His dominion over sin.

We learn that He entered battle as a warrior King to gain that right. Look at the words in verse 5: "One of the elders said . . . , 'Behold, the Lion of the tribe of Judah, the Root of David, has prevailed to open the scroll.'" "The Lion of the tribe of Judah, the Root of David" sounds nice, but the language is more than poetic. It reflects on history and then makes a prophecy out of the context of that historic observation.

The history was this: the tribe of Judah was the largest tribe in terms of its furnishing troops in ancient Israel. Anytime that we read the numberings of the tribes and their hosts for battle in the Old Testament, we see that Judah had the largest host. We also know that they were always the ones who strategically led forth in battle. They were the troops at the head of the army. The tribe of Judah had a banner with a lion on it; that was the symbol of their tribe. The grandest moments of the tribe of Judah and of all the people of Israel occurred during that season of time when David was the king of Israel.

Under David's leadership, two things took place. First, all oppression that had come against Israel was broken and driven back. Even the relentless Philistines, who seemed to ceaselessly come wave upon wave, were driven back. Second—and this is the big one—David extended the boundaries of Israel to the widest dimensions in the nation's history. David broke the power of oppression and opened up dimensions of possibility that the people had never known before. There is a message for you and me.

The reference to Jesus as the Lion of the tribe of Judah means that He has come to break the back of what oppresses and to open up dimensions of possibility that have not been known before because mankind has never had a chance to test the possibilities of the will of God.

Then John said, "And I looked." What would you have thought to see? Perhaps you would picture a great prince on a white horse in gleaming battle armor and banners arrayed around him. But John saw One that was like a Lamb. The description of "a Lamb as though it had been slain" literally is translated "bearing the marks of recent slaughter."

Some time ago, I presented a series on the ascended Christ to my church. I turned to Revelation 5 and noted that there is strong evidence that this passage records the moment that Jesus first stepped back into heaven, having returned from earth at the time of the Ascension—following His death and resurrection.

On the Lamb "bearing the marks of slaughter," the remaining signs of angry wounds were still freshly visible. They were healed, but they were recent. You may say, "Wait just a minute. How can that be since John saw this vision in A.D. 80 or 85?"

But remember, when John stepped through that door into the presence of God, he stepped into eternity, the realm of timelessness. Just as he was about to view events thousands of years in the future, he could equally look back at events that took place half a century before. In the realm of timelessness, he was unrestricted by his immediate time frame. So he saw the warrior King who has gained the right to take the scroll.

We are reminded upon the Lamb's arrival how His victory was achieved through the Cross! We are not shown a mighty King upon a horse, but a slaughtered Lamb—the Lamb of God who "takes away the sin of the world." The Lamb did not need to suffer one thing by reason of His own guilt or shame: He had none. But He voluntarily took our place. The One who took the scroll is the One who so loved us that He endured what He did for the sake of bringing about the release of mankind's salvation—and the hope of restoring human destiny . . . one by one.

It is a price none of us can fathom. The only way we can begin to understand is to weigh it in terms of an individual's private suffering. Our Savior bore upon His shoulders all the guilt of all humanity from all history. The sinless Son of God, who from eternity had known unbroken fellowship with the Father, experienced this coming upon Him; His relationship with the Father was severed as He took our place and bore our curse. His victory was achieved through the Cross as the Lamb. And that is what we learn with the Lamb's arrival at the throne.

SIGNIFICANT INSIGHTS

What insights, then, do we gain from the whole scenario? First, this whole scenario shows us that God is a good God, and His will is benevolent. He has been holding in trust a violated gift that He willed for mankind's blessing on earth. And when man violated the terms of that covenant, God did not simply tear up the scroll and say, "I've got nothing to do with you."

He doesn't do that personally, either. God doesn't shred His purpose for or commitment to you or me, despite our failures. He still has hold of it! Though it may be riddled with curse, and the liar-thief is having his heyday, God still says, "I am not going to let this go or them go. I am going to patiently prepare their time of redemption." Listen, let Him speak to you: "Never forget that I never meant for your struggle to be the way it has become. I want instead what is going to be, and in the meantime My Son will attend your way if you will allow Him." Yes, this scenario displays the fact that God is a good God, and His will is benevolent.

Second, this scenario shows us that the Cross can break any curse. Jesus Christ stepped into human history and turned the tide of everything so that eventually there will be the revoking of evil's sway and a resolution of history; a purpose with the triumph of God's will and purpose for mankind and this planet. If He can do that with all human history, let me suggest that He can manage your life too. Since the Cross has broken the death grip that Satan has on the planet, it can break any grip that hell has on you or me. Praise God!

Third, this scenario shows us that all prayer will be answered. Verse 8 notes the bowls of incense filled with the prayers of the saints, which we discussed earlier. People usually say there are three answers to prayer: yes, no, or later. But there is another. Many "yes" answers weren't noticed; we didn't recognize them because they weren't the answers we wanted. Prayers come before the throne of God, all are received, and there is in heaven a store of the prayers that haven't happened yet. In chapter 8, these prayers are being poured out, and something begins to happen as a result of these prayers in a huge bowl. The consummation of all things will come about as a combination of God's saying, "There will be delay no longer," and people having prayed, "Father, let Your kingdom come in its ultimate sense." Their prayers will be answered.

This has its personal way of happening too. Many years ago Anna and I became very, very concerned about a circumstance involving a family member, one fraught with great difficulty. The details are too complex to tell, but about four years ago the Lord whispered to my wife one day, "Pray this way . . ." We had been praying, but here was discernment of *how* to pray about the situation. So we did—we started praying that way, specifically, at least three or four times per week, thinking the results would occur soon. But a year went by, and then another year. We didn't stop praying because we had the Lord's specific direction, but we were surprised by the lack of visible results.

Then one day last spring, it happened! It happened so fast that we thought, *It didn't really happen, did it?* But it really did! And it happened so dramatically, we then thought, *Is it going to last?* But time has proven all: the Lord broke the chains of the situation. And what was happening in the meantime—when nothing seemed to be happening? Hear me: every one of those prayers was being gathered in heaven—as incense, just as John describes before the throne of God.

So whatever you are praying for, when it doesn't seem to be happening, know that heaven is not going to leave any prayer unanswered. All prayers are presently retained before the throne of God. They are much more than sweet smelling; they are a worship expression of dependence upon God. So keep praying.

Fourth, this scenario shows us what it means to praise. When those beings begin to praise around the throne and then the ripples of praise go out in concentric circles until praise encompasses the earth, including you and me, that praise is not waiting until the accomplishment of the deal. If the Lamb is in action; everything's in motion. It's just a matter of time now! Here is the grand reason for praise, for God's will is now in the process of being recovered through His Son.

As we look at this text and see the scroll, the centerpiece of the book of Revelation, its application is personal in very real ways, and it is panoramic in others. But all of it welds together to say, "Praise the Lord because He is good. Praise Him because Jesus is Lord and He is at work. Praise Him because He is coming again, and there will be the ultimate realization of these things." In the meantime, He comes into our circumstances with transforming power. You have experienced it before, there will be more, and there will be the ultimate as well. All this and heaven too.

7

In the Light of the E Quake

REVELATION 6:1–17

We are coming to what I believe is the key to unlocking the book of Revelation and to clarifying its content in its applicability to us today. The book of Revelation was not given to us as a book for speculation. It was not given as a coffee table book for the saints to sit around and talk about because it would be "fun to guess." It was given for very pragmatic reasons: to encourage in the midst of trial, to motivate in the time of opportunity, to bring us to worship and praise before the Lord, and to realize that in the spirit of praise around His timeless throne, there is constantly an unscrolling of God's purpose in motion, which is worldwide, yet personal in its implications.

Now I saw when the Lamb opened one of the seals; and I heard one of the four living creatures saying with a voice like

111

thunder, "Come and see." And I looked, and behold, a white horse. He who sat on it had a bow; and a crown was given to him, and he went out conquering and to conquer. When He opened the second seal, I heard the second living creature saying, "Come and see." Another horse, fiery red, went out. And it was granted to the one who sat on it to take peace from the earth, and that people should kill one another; and there was given to him a great sword. When He opened the third seal, I heard the third living creature say, "Come and see." So I looked, and behold, a black horse, and he who sat on it had a pair of scales in his hand. And I heard a voice in the midst of the four living creatures saying, "A quart of wheat for a denarius, and three quarts of barley for a denarius; and do not harm the oil and the wine." (Rev. 6:1–6)

These verses announce that in the midst of affluence, there would still be amazing and desperate need for the basic staff of life. A quart of wheat would sell for a day's wage (a denarius was a day's wage in that time). There would be plenty of the oil and the wine, which would depict the luxurious, the extra, but the basic thing that you need, the wheat, is out of reach. A famine has brought things to such a point that there are still many of the accoutrements of luxury but not the practical needs for basic nourishment.

When He opened the fourth seal, I heard the voice of the fourth living creature saying, "Come and see." So I looked, and behold, a pale horse. And the name of him who sat on it was Death, and Hades followed with him. And power was given to them over a fourth of the earth, to kill with sword, with hunger, with death, and by the beasts of the earth. When He opened the fifth seal, I saw under the altar the souls of those who had been slain for the word of God and for the testimony which they held. And they cried with a loud voice, saying, "How long, O Lord, holy and true, until You judge and avenge our blood on those who dwell on the earth?" Then a white robe was given to each of them; and it was said to them that they should rest a little while longer, until both the number of their fellow servants and their brethren, who would be killed as they were, was completed. (Rev. 6:7–11)

Notice there are two groups: those who would not necessarily experience martyrdom would complete the number coming into redemption's circle as well as those who died for their faith.

I looked when He opened the sixth seal, and behold, there was a great earthquake; and the sun became black as sackcloth of hair, and the moon became like blood. And the stars of heaven fell to the earth, as a fig tree drops its late figs when it is shaken by a mighty wind. Then the sky receded as a scroll when it is rolled up, and every mountain and island was moved out of its place. And the kings of the earth, the great men, the rich men, the commanders, the mighty men, every slave and every free man, hid themselves in the caves and in the rocks of the mountains, and said to the mountains and rocks, "Fall on us and hide us from the face of Him who sits on the throne and from the wrath of the Lamb! For the great day of His wrath has come, and who is able to stand?" (Rev. 6:12–17)

It may seem innocuous to begin a discussion of such a crucial and dramatic passage by referring to a football team. From my high school years and right up to today, I have been very, very interested in football. I used to play a lot. I also read books pertaining to the history of football. Most people have heard the name of Knute Rockne, who was the coach at Notre Dame until his tragic, early death in an airplane accident. The team was the powerhouse of the nation in the late 1920s and the 1930s. After the team rolled up one victory after another, the renowned sportswriter of that era, Grantland Rice, established a piece of prose that is quoted to this day by people who know the game. He penned these words after another victory with Notre Dame's remarkable backfield and four players who were the strong front line: "Under a gray October sky, the four horsemen rode again." Rice was taking the figure of the passage we have just read and saying that just as the passage of Scripture depicted horrendous devastation and irresistible forces, so the team had a devastating effect on other teams.

THE JUDGMENTS

This passage launches us into the portion of the book of Revelation that most people think about when reading Revelation—the judgments. The judgments unscroll as Jesus Himself begins to break the seals that there might come the ultimate revealing of the will of God on earth. Remember that judgment is not the desire of God or even His will in terms of what He would most wish—the restoration of the benevolent intent of Father God.

God never intended for anything to be as it has become. These judgments never would have been necessary were it not for human sin giving place to the horrendous works of hell. In order for all of this to be flushed out, we see the Lamb—who has come to the throne and stood before the Father, having accomplished the work of redemption at the Cross and risen—taking the scroll and breaking the seals. This is a very pivotal place to be because as the indescribable, horrible things happened upon the earth, the Lamb of God presided over the events with the breaking of each seal.

I want to call your attention to a number of things in this chapter. We are going to conclude by looking at the passage we just read where this last earthquake occurs. I call it the E Quake, just as I referred to the scroll that is being opened as the E Book. The E Quake is the end event of this world as we know it.

As we look at life in that light, recall what Peter said in one of his epistles, "Since all these things will be dissolved, what manner of persons ought [we] to be?" (2 Peter 3:11). Francis Schaeffer was a well-known thinker/philosopher in the name of Christ, who influenced many people. Schaeffer wrote the book *How Should We Then Live?* Even if we never read the book, the title is enough to summon us to think in these terms. That idea is set forward as we begin the unscrolling.

A WAKE-UP CALL

Jesus is sending out a wake-up call. An announcement comes with the breaking of each seal. John wrote, "Now I saw when the Lamb opened one of the seals; and I heard one of the four living creatures saying with a voice like thunder, 'Come and see'" (6:1). The mighty cherubim around the throne announce something profound.

We have seen these beings in chapters 4 and 5. They are around the throne of almighty God, Creator and Father, and they constantly bow before Him, saying, "Holy, holy, holy, Lord God Almighty."

Here, however, the beings are not bowed toward the throne; they are turned out toward John. They call to him as the Lamb takes the scroll. Something dramatic in both this postural and this verbal change occurs. By turning to speak to John—and thereby speaking to you and me, to the people of God—they are not at this moment worshiping God. Momentarily they turn from that worship to say, "There is something that you need to capture." In other words, this is more than a scene of worship; it is a scene of mission that is being established and released—right now. They are saying, "Something is going to happen in your world. Come and see what is ahead for your world." The seals begin to break, and we are shown a series of things.

John said, "I saw one on a white horse going forth with a bow, a crown on his head, conquering and to conquer." That is the first. Seals two, three, and four all have to do with devastating things that impact the earth with death, famine, and all manner of grief. Number five, which really ties in to number one as we will shortly see, has to do with a group of people who have borne the testimony of Christ and who are crying and wondering how long it will be until He comes again. How much longer must the suffering go on, especially the suffering experienced by their peers in time and people who share the faith throughout the course of history, those who have been martyred for their faith and have been persecuted.

In our nation, even the worst persecution we face is nothing compared to that faced by hundreds of thousands of brothers and sisters in Christ around the world. There are more Christians being persecuted for their faith than people of any other tradition in the world, and there is less said on their behalf.

The sixth seal is a horrendous earthquake. In the light of that quake, which is the end of everything—and I will qualify that—we are called to "come and see."

One Woman's Response

Anna and I were on a cruise with a couple of hundred people from the radio and television ministry as well as some people from our church one summer. We met a woman from our group who shared with us her quest for the will of God in her life. As we were speaking together, she also explained a little bit about her background. We immediately had the sense that she was an extraordinarily gifted person. We could not help being impressed. It was really rather moving to hear someone say exactly what she was saying. In the position she held as an executive in a corporation, the name of which you would recognize, she had seven thousand people accountable to her.

She was in her mid-forties, I suppose, and with all the recognition, the accoutrements of success surrounding her, she said, "Pastor Jack, I wanted to talk to you and Anna for just a few moments because the Lord has been dealing with my heart in a most profound way. Many of my friends say, 'Keep doing what you are doing because you are such a strong witness with your influence in the corporation.'" She was feeling a sense of God's direction for her to enter some phase of Christian leadership. To leave the security, the very fine salary, all the extras associated with her position—and it was not as though she would enter a life of poverty—would be a big step. She would apply all of her resources to an entirely different arena of life and service—answering the call of Jesus.

I want to say before I go any farther, I am not suggesting that what she was being called to do is what everybody ought to consider, as though the calling were more noble than others. Many of us who lead in the body of Christ are finding more and more people who are coming to a place where they have achieved much in their lives and they are seeking beyond their success to find another dimension of significance—moving from success to significance. It is not as though their lives have been insignificant to this point, but they are feeling a sense of a call to a different dimension of significance.

As she spoke with us, it was not a matter of my saying the religious, correct thing because I don't consider it correct. I don't consider it more godly to serve in a spiritual or sacred environment, a church ministry, than to serve Jesus in any other place that He puts a person. But it became very clear to Anna and me that indeed, the Holy Spirit was calling her *unto* a place of ministry.

I would never use whatever influence the Lord gives me in a person's life to emphasize something that life changing and transforming with such pressure that the individual would feel obligated to do it because "Pastor Jack suggested it." I didn't suggest it in the first place, but even if I confirmed it, she might consider that to have authority. I told her, "You need to talk to your pastor."

She called later to say that she had talked with her pastor. She laughed when she told us, "The first thing he did was start laughing and say, 'Wake up and smell the coffee. God's calling you.'" There was something about that sense of confirmation to her. She knew the Lord was saying to her, "Come and see."

Jesus is sending out a wake-up call everywhere today. Whether or not it effects a change in a person's vocation isn't the point; the point is, we are being called to decide "what manner of persons ought we to be?" Notwithstanding our own set of woes personally, nationally, or economically, as the case may be, they are nothing compared to the needs in the world around us. At the very outset of this unscrolling of the will of God during this age we call the church age, the breaking of the seals is not something that takes place in the distant future; it is not something that took place in the past; it is something that is opening during the age we are going through now. It is an era in which a number of things are happening, as this scroll outlines, which then will come to a climax.

One on a White Horse

The angelic creatures around the throne that direct worship to God turn, seeming to say, "As you worship Him, *Come and see!*" The first thing that we see as the scroll breaks is a picture. It is a picture of one on a white horse going forth with a crown on his head and a bow in his hand, conquering and to conquer.

Most commentaries offer two points on this. One view is

that Jesus Himself is described. The argument against this being Jesus is made by those who say, "Why does He have a bow in His hand instead of a sword? And why does He have one crown instead of many crowns as described in chapter 19? How could this possibly be Jesus?"

The Lamb is at the beginning of His crusade to touch the world. The bow reminds us of God being like a Father who takes His children as arrows in a quiver. To Father God, His children are like arrows that He sends on missions. And Jesus comes with a bow to take His own, commission them, and send them, like arrows, to various places of ministry. That can be touching people in your neighborhood or touching people in the farthest corner of the earth. Jesus comes with a single crown because it is the beginning—the crown He has received through His triumph of the Cross. He will gain crown upon crown upon crown as triumph follows triumph follows triumph. He goes forth on a white horse that is representative of the righteous leadership of our Savior conquering and to conquer. His kingdom is beginning to spread—the glorious growth and expansion of His kingdom rule.

On to Victory

In that breaking of the first seal is the picture of Jesus leading His own to victory. In the fifth seal is a companion to this; movement toward victory is not superficial triumphalism. Don't make any mistake, loved one. While the Church does move in triumph, there is a concept that though we are people of triumph, we have not been called to victory. Some people have the notion that we are supposed to have ceaseless strings of victories, but there is no such thing as a victory without a battle. There is no such thing as a battle without casualties. The idea that the Church is called to a rose-strewn pathway of victory to victory mistakes the point. My pastor used to say years ago, "Yes, this is a pathway of roses, but please remember, there are many thorns too." The difference here is that triumphalism is the notion that there is no such thing as a trial or a struggle or a casualty in the pathway toward Christian roses. But we experience trial and difficulty, and some people lose their lives.

I received word from my friend Lloyd Ogilvie's office one day that Senator Lieberman had presented before the Senate a bill to bring about an activism on the part of our nation to defend against the anti-Christian bias that is creeping in, almost with impunity, in many parts of the world today. It is amazing to me how human rights can be argued for every environment unless a person is a Christian and then he has no human rights. I think the proposed bill is good news, not because we beg relief from persecution, but because the more opportunity there is for a voice to be raised in the name of Jesus, then the more people will come to know His love and His life.

We Christians will never completely escape persecution. There is no prophecy that suggests it, and it is not a matter of whimpering and whining because it happens. It is simply saying what is good for the goose is good for the gander. If we are called to be protective of human rights in any environment, then there ought to be equal rights provided for Christians throughout the world as well. That issue is being argued favorably right now. Notwithstanding those things of political action, the long-range result inevitably will be as it has always been through Church history. I am not being fatalistic—I am being realistic—people will die for their faith.

THE CALL OF GOD AND YOUNG PEOPLE

Anna and I were in Tucson where we spoke to more than seven hundred leaders who were gathered there from one of the districts of our denomination. Joining me on the speaking team was an elder of our congregation, Jim Tolle, who has served as the head of the global missions ministry of an entire denomination that reaches into more than one hundred nations. Last year more than a half million decisions for Jesus Christ were recorded through the outreach of the churches in that ministry. Jim and Alice are a part of our church family and used to be on our church staff years ago. Jim discussed something that he is encountering as he moves from state to state and from nation to nation. People are constantly talking to him about vision and things God is putting on their hearts. Speaking to pastors, he said with tears in his eyes, "Brothers and sisters, please talk with your young people about this."

Jim cited the frequency with which young people come up to him and say, "The Lord is calling to me." Then they name a nation that is hostile to the gospel of Jesus Christ: places in China, Pakistan, Bangladesh, the Middle East, or Africa. This is not something they have invented of their own minds.

Jim said, "This is the thing that I lament. These kids have a call of God on their hearts and can tell you that with crystal clarity in their eyes. They are not fanatics; they are not idiots; they are young people with a sense of life call and mission. But when a young person tells his parents that he feels called to a nation, at first the parents are rather casual in their response. The more the young person says, 'Mom, Dad, God is saying this to me,' the less support he gets until finally the line is drawn in the sand. The parents say, 'Do you think we are going to give you a college or university education so you can go there and die?'" He wept. He continued, "Please ask our people to make a decision. Who and what are we as the people of God?" I heard in his voice a being from around the throne saying to us, "Come and see."

There is One going forth conquering and to conquer, and there will be those who give their lives for the sake of the gospel. But in the last analysis, loved one, as long ago was said in a speech that we all revere because of what it meant to our nation's ultimate liberty, "Is life so dear?" There are souls that need to be unchained.

In the years that I was involved in recruiting for our college when I served as director of college relations and dean of students, I found the attitude that Jim mentioned. But it wasn't so much an issue of persecution and the possible death of a child who would answer the call of God and some years later go to preach the gospel in a hostile environment. It was more an issue of economic undesirability verbalized in the question, "Why would any person want to train for ministry?"

Parents would say to a young person, "Why don't you first go to a [they never said the word *real* but that was what they meant] college so that you have an education, something [are you ready for this] to fall back on?"

Dear one, when I was a senior in high school, I was one of the top students. Most of the teachers tried to dissuade me from a call to go to a little "nothing" LIFE Bible College in Los Angeles, a pentecostal college at that. The homeroom teacher for my class, Helen Voekel, was a Lutheran, born-again believer who loved Jesus Christ, and she encouraged me. Mrs. Voekel said, "Jack, I understand what it means when you say God has called you. Hang tough there, son." I understand the value system of our world, but this message has to do with our kids and God's calling kids. God is saying, "I want to do something in your world."

ULTIMATE HOPE AND JOY

Then these beings call out three times in succession, "Come and see; come and see; come and see." And we come to the next series of things—Jesus reminding us that the roots of hope and joy can never find their fullest nourishment in the soil of this planet. See, we want to protect ourselves from answering whatever call God would put upon us or our children and just have nice lives. I'm not presuming God's call always contains tragedy. I'm simply saying that life needs to be seen realistically and with eternity's values in view.

He opens the second seal—a fiery red horse—and there is no peace on earth. He opens another seal, and there is famine (6:5–6). He opens another seal, and there is death everywhere by many means (6:7–8).

Today, read Matthew 24 and Luke 21 sometime before you go to bed. It will not take very long. You will be reading about Jesus on either Monday or Tuesday before He died on the cross. He was on the Mount of Olives from which He could see the overview of the temple grounds. The disciples had heard Jesus say that those things would one day not be there, and they asked, "When will these things be? And what will be the sign of Your coming, and of the end of the age?" (Matt. 24:3).

They had the same questions that we have about how all of this will come to a climax. Jesus sat down with them and began to spell it out in what is called the Olivet Discourse. He said, "See not all these things." In other words, the roots of what hope and fulfillment and joy we have are never going to find nourishment sunk in the soil of this planet.

Loved one, I am not arguing against the possibilities of a happy life. I am not arguing against enjoying things. I occasionally play a round of golf. I enjoy it a lot. Anna and I had an opportunity while in Arizona to make a quick trip to Sedona. I had never seen the majesty of the Red Rocks of Sedona. Everybody ought to have a chance to see them. There are beautiful things to enjoy and pleasures to be known on this earth. I am not talking about a monastic appeal to godliness; I am talking about keeping a perspective on what it means to be the people of God in a time like ours.

The whole point of this passage of Scripture in light of these horrendous things that are cited is that they are agelong. The seals go on during this whole era. Jesus said the same thing in those passages I would like for you to read. He mentioned wars and rumors of wars, tribulation, earthquakes, famines. He said, "And when these things are going on, this isn't the end yet." These things will happen. He said, "They are going to persecute you for My name's sake. Error is going to run rampant." He went through a list of things. And His purpose was not to create

125

a group of disciples with dour faces. He wanted to bring about a people who had the solid view that they were not going to derive a sense of hope and joy by becoming dependent upon the things of this world.

The world is a nice place to be at many locations, at many times, and it is not unworthy to enjoy some of these things. But if you are looking for long-term joy, plant your roots in Glory.

A COSMIC EVENT

Revelation 6:12–17 describes the last great event of this world as we know it: the earthquake. However, it is not the last great event of this world.

Later in the book, we will deal with this earthquake as it occurs elsewhere in the book of Revelation. There are five mentions of earthquakes in Revelation. I believe that the book of Revelation offers different viewpoints on the same earthquake, and I think that this belief can be verified. If there are two earthquakes, one begins and then a short time later there is a horrendous aftershock.

We read, "Then the sky receded as a scroll when it is rolled up, and every mountain and island was moved out of its place" (6:14). This earthquake is more than a seismic event. Every island and mountain moved out of its place. This is not simply a buildup of forces of tectonic plates followed by an explosion in some location. Even if we had a horrendous earthquake that circled the whole Pacific Rim, which is known to be seismically active, that would not move every mountain and island out of its place.

We are talking about a cosmic event. It has seismic implications; it changes the face of the planet. Simultaneous with this occurrence, I believe the Bible reveals that this is when the Rapture takes place.

I want to talk more about the Rapture and this earthquake later on. But right now, I want you to see that it is unstraining the text of Revelation as well as simplifying the whole of the book to realize that it is one great end time quake with five different perspectives on it. There is no question that such an earthquake would be cosmic.

Isn't it remarkable that as we approach a time in history when so many other issues of Bible prophecy are coming about, the world of science has come to some of the same convictions? This has occurred in the last ten years. I have done quite a bit of reading on this particular subject of a convergence of interests by geologists and astronomers. They have studied things that they can see of the devastating events in the past of our planet's geophysical history, and many of them contend that we are headed for such an encounter again. You've read about ongoing studies, and Hollywood is catching up with the scientific research and producing movies with titles such as *Deep Impact* and *Armageddon*. The question is not *if* but *when* an asteroid or a comet will strike our planet.

Multiplied hundreds of people—all over this planet—will be out tonight with equipment that has never been available before with such precision and efficiency at a price that they can afford. There will be people on rooftops and in forests. Some will be professionals, but most will be well-trained amateurs, scanning the skies to see if they can find yet-unrecognized comets or asteroids. Many of these objects have never been identified.

So far more than four hundred earth-orbit-intersecting aster-oids have been identified. That means there is a point that their orbit intersects ours. The good news is that most of them—in fact, all of them so far—don't have a projected time when an orbit intersection would occasion a collision. However, a few years ago an asteroid passed within 65,000 miles of earth. In cosmic pro-portions that is called a bullet burn—having your scalp grazed.

This is not anything new to anybody. But I bring it up because we are living in a time when the world is waking up to the fact that this is real and that this is not just a horrendous vision, an apocalyptic nightmare that somebody had one night. So if anyone happens to see or has seen *Deep Impact* or *Armageddon,* remember that the ancient pages of God's Word rise to say, *"You heard it here first!"*

THE RIGHT PRIORITIES

In light of this discussion, "what manner of persons ought [we] to be?" Jesus is pointing toward a dramatic and drastic climax to history, one that is being brought to our attention right now. But it is not just being brought to our attention by astronomers and geologists; it is being brought to our attention by the Holy Spirit, who is saying, "Seeing that all these things are ultimately going to be gone, what manner of persons ought we to be?" Running scared? No. Retreating from life and drawing up in a corner to think godly thoughts while we wait for the world to come to an end? No. Not enjoying anything of life? Oh, Jesus came to give us life—and life abundantly. What then? Be sure your value system is clear and your priorities are right.

The King is going forth conquering and to conquer. I suggest that first, we line up with Him, take our swords, and let Him take each one of us as an arrow, string us, and direct us toward what He wants to do with us. If God moves on you and says, "I want to alter what you are doing with your life," don't do it as a religious pursuit; do it as a person commissioned under God's grace to do the next happy thing in your life. If God moves your kids and calls them, hold your children with an open hand submitted to the will of God.

When those cherubim say, "Come and see," and show Jesus going forth conquering first and then three horrendous things, they are not saying, "Come and look at the mess. Come and look at the famines. Come and look at the dying. Come and look at the war." The angelic beings are saying, "First, Jesus is going forth leading His people, conquering and to conquer, and He is calling them to look and see that there is a world fraught with famine, bloodshed, war, and death. That is where you are being sent to go with the love and life of Jesus." Don't just look and say, "Well, there are horrible things prophesied for earth." Take note that these things are prophesied so that you and I would recognize that that is the arena of our mission and lives. We go with the love of God and the life of God and in the name of Jesus. Let's look at Revelation not as a book of speculation about events in the future, but as a book that calls us to the realization of what we were made to be in Christ.

If you have never come to know Jesus Christ, the Word of God appeals to you, "Come and see." Look at events in the past, and open your eyes and see where the Son of God died for you and for me on the cross. You are the same as I am. You are a sinner who needs a Savior, and you need to come to Jesus so that your heart is aligned with the love of God, coming to embrace Him who is reaching to embrace you. Begin life that has its purpose and richness now so that there is not any defeat in any circumstance. You are riding with One who is going forth conquering and to conquer. You move with Him.

8

REVELATION AND THE RAPTURE

REVELATION 7

After these things I looked, and behold, a great multitude which no one could number, of all nations, tribes, peoples, and tongues, standing before the throne and before the Lamb, clothed with white robes, with palm branches in their hands, and crying out with a loud voice, saying, "Salvation belongs to our God who sits on the throne, and to the Lamb!" All the angels stood around the throne and the elders and the four living creatures, and fell on their faces before the throne and worshiped God, saying,

"Amen! Blessing and glory and wisdom,
Thanksgiving and honor and power and might,
Be to our God forever and ever. Amen."

Then one of the elders answered, saying to me, "Who are these arrayed in white robes, and where did they come from?" And

I said to him, "Sir, you know." So he said to me, "These are the ones who come out of the great tribulation, and washed their robes and made them white in the blood of the Lamb. Therefore they are before the throne of God, and serve Him day and night in His temple. And He who sits on the throne will dwell among them. They shall neither hunger anymore nor thirst anymore; the sun shall not strike them, nor any heat; for the Lamb who is in the midst of the throne will shepherd them and lead them to living fountains of waters. And God will wipe away every tear from their eyes." (Rev. 7:9–17)

Three or four years ago a very gifted vocalist from our congregation was ministering in a church in San Francisco. Steve Amerson told me the following story of how the pastor was speaking on the return of the Lord Jesus Christ from heaven. As he concluded the first service, a young woman, who had received Jesus not many weeks before, came up to him. She was so deeply moved that she said to the pastor, "Pastor, this morning, I can't tell you how thrilling it is to me! As you know, I just received Jesus, but until this morning I didn't know that the One who came and died on the cross to save me and rose from the dead and went to heaven was coming back again." It was such a precious thing to her to hear that Jesus is coming back. Jesus is coming again.

THE PROMISE OF JESUS' RETURN

In the New Testament there are approximately 180 chapters. On the average, there are as many references to the second coming of Jesus as there are chapters. I didn't say there is a reference in every chapter; there is not.

His return is as clear as anything in the world, and it has been enunciated first and foremost by the Savior Himself. On the night before He was crucified, Jesus spoke to the disciples, who observed His dour countenance (they were not aware that the Cross would occur within hours). Sensing their dismay, Jesus said,

> Let not your heart be troubled; you believe in God, believe also in Me. In My Father's house are many mansions; if it were not so, I would have told you. I go to prepare a place for you. And if I go and prepare a place for you, I will come again and receive you to Myself; that where I am, there you may be also. (John 14:1–2)

It is a personal promise to every one of us, a promise of the Lord's coming and taking us to a specific place. As it has often been said, "Heaven is a prepared place for a prepared people."

The next day when He was on trial, Jesus stood before His critics, the ones who designed His crucifixion. They screamed at Him, "Are You the Christ, the Son of the Blessed?" Jesus answered them unabashedly and forthrightly, "I am." And He went farther, "And you will see the Son of Man sitting at the right hand of the Power, and coming with the clouds of heaven" (Mark 14:61–62). He told them that He was the Christ, that He would rule from the right hand of Father God, and that He would come again from heaven.

On the day that Jesus ascended, only weeks following the Resurrection, the Bible says that He was caught up out of their midst. As they stood there gazing up into the sky, suddenly two angelic beings appeared and said to them, "Men of Galilee, why do you stand gazing up into heaven? This same Jesus . . . will so come [listen to these words] in like manner as you saw Him go into heaven" (Acts 1:11). Same Jesus, in like manner as you saw Him go. In other words, this is not a substitute return; it is not in the person of someone else. Never be deceived by that. Never have the notion that it is somebody who seems like Jesus. He warned that people would say, "Here is Christ and there is Christ," and they would deceive many. This same Jesus will come in the same manner that you saw Him go. He literally, physically, ascended to heaven in the clouds. He literally, physically, will return, as the Scripture says, with the clouds.

THE RAPTURE

We are looking at the Revelation and the Rapture, and as we do, I want to look at the coming of Christ and the "catching away" into His presence of the people who have put their faith in Him. As we are "caught away" into His presence, the word commonly used in the life of the Church to describe the instant translation from here to there is *Rapture*. It has been used in our language for centuries. However, the word *Rapture* does not occur in the Bible.

The Rapture is wrapped up in all the things that are inherent in a Greek word translated "caught up" to be together with the Lord. It is the word *harpazo*. Harpazo has three basic ideas, and interestingly enough, since the word is used thirteen times in the Greek New Testament, there are illustrations of each shade of meaning. Let's examine the three meanings.

SEIZED SUDDENLY

The first is "to seize with a sudden and overwhelming force," much as an eagle would come down from the sky and snatch its prey, then take it back to its nest. It is much the same as a predator would pursue another animal and then leap upon it, flay its flesh, bite into its throat, and tear it apart. It is a vicious idea in terms of the suddenness and the seizure involved.

The concept in the Rapture is not destructive in that sense, but it is the suddenness of it and the taking away with rapidity. *Harpazo* is used this way in John 10 where Jesus described His own as sheep and the adversary like a wolf who comes to steal, to kill, and to destroy. Satan comes at people that way.

You may be reading this right now and thinking that you have been assailed, ripped, and torn—even faster than you could have braced yourself—by an assault of the devil. Some people bear a scar all the way to the present as a result of a past experience. You could be in the forty-fifth year of your life, and you still suffer from something that happened to you forty years ago—and there came the ripping and the tearing.

But there is a blessed aspect of this; there will come a sudden appearance of Jesus from heaven. There will not be the kind of Rapture that sometimes is depicted in artistry. I have seen paintings of people floating up through the sky. No one is going to see anybody floating up in the sky.

It is going to happen the way a young man described to me recently after a service. He said, "Pastor, whenever I think of the Rapture now, I think of something I saw at an air show this summer. We were all lined up in stands, thousands of us seated there, and suddenly, we could see a jet aircraft less than fifty feet off the ground going full tilt. It went by so fast that the eye could hardly follow. You didn't hear the roar until it was past because of its speed, but then there was a thunderous roar in its wake. When you looked again, it was gone. That's the way I think of the Rapture." I said, "Thank you for that imagery because that's exactly the way to describe it."

TRANSPORTED

The second meaning is of "being transported to another setting." The Bible says there will be an awesome power that instantly—in a moment, in the twinkling of an eye—transports us to another place. Jesus said, "I will bring you to the place I have prepared for you."

The story of the evangelist Philip is found in Acts 8. After he had a great meeting in Samaria, the Lord told him to go out in the desert. The instructions didn't make sense since things were going so well in Samaria. The fact of the matter is that Philip's moving into the desert brought about an intersection with a man traveling with an entourage because of his high position in the court of Ethiopia. He was on his way back, reading from a scroll of Isaiah. Philip, who had been hiking through the desert, saw the chariot coming, and the man asked Philip to come into the chariot. The Ethiopian was reading from Isaiah 53 but didn't understand it. Philip interpreted the passage, and the man came to understand who Jesus was as Messiah and opened his heart to the Savior. When they came upon an oasis, Philip baptized the man. Right after that, Philip was suddenly caught away, gone. It is one of the miracles of the New Testament that is least talked about. The next thing anyone knew, Philip was in Azotus. He had hiked out to the desert, but suddenly, he was transported to another place. It was a supernatural removal from the situation.

I thought about that incident after reading the text again as I prepared for this book. I had never thought about it before, but I dare say that the Ethiopian probably thought that Philip was an angel because of the sudden disappearance of the man. In any case, it is the idea of suddenly being transported, the sudden overwhelming force that transports one to another setting. We will suddenly be in glory. The Bible says, "And so shall we ever be with the Lord."

RESCUED

The third meaning of *harpazo* is "to seize and rescue from imminent peril." In the story of Paul's revisiting of Jerusalem (Acts 23), a mob assailed him. Two factions had a hold of opposite sides of his body and were about to literally rip and tear him apart. But a Roman cohort moved in and rescued Paul. It was one of those "within an inch of your life" kind of things. The word used in Acts when they took Paul means that they literally seized him from the people. It was a rescue event, which is the third of three things describing the Rapture to us.

The Rapture will happen in a sudden action that can be likened only to a violent attack. We usually think of something rapturous as being magnificently and overwhelmingly uplifting and exhilarating. Yet it is related to the word *raptor,* which is a beast of prey that rips and tears the flesh. The suddenness is the part that is related. It is taking out of imminent peril, or danger, that brings us to the time of the Rapture in the light of the Word of God.

THE SIXTH SEAL

This passage we are reading is set in more than one perspective. We have discussed that the book of Revelation becomes distorted when a linear approach is taken. It is easy to become confused with this approach because the book of Revelation is not written in a linear fashion. It is a series of prophecies that are seen from different viewpoints. As we look from the different viewpoints, a clearer picture is painted for us. The Rapture is mentioned in three other places in Revelation.

We learned of the great earthquake in Revelation 6:12–17. The opening of the sixth seal is really the last. There is a seventh seal, but it opens the trumpets and the bowls that bring the concluding events. The seventh trumpet, which is born out of this immediate sequence of events, is critical to this issue of time.

Let's reread these verses: "I looked when He opened the sixth seal, and behold, there was a great earthquake; and the sun became black as sackcloth of hair, and the moon became like blood. And the stars of heaven fell to the earth, as a fig tree drops its late figs when it is shaken by a mighty wind" (Rev. 6:12–13).

In Matthew 24:29–31, Jesus answered the disciples' question regarding the sign of His coming and of the end. These are the words of Jesus:

> Immediately after the tribulation of those days the sun will be darkened, and the moon will not give its light; the stars will fall from heaven, and the powers of the heavens will be shaken. Then the sign of the Son of Man will appear in heaven, and then all the tribes of the earth will mourn, and they will see the Son of Man coming on the clouds of heaven with power and great glory. And He will send His angels with a great sound of a trumpet, and they will gather together His elect from the four winds, from one end of heaven to the other.

The sound of a trumpet comes immediately in the wake of these cosmically disturbing events, which occasion the darkening of the sun and the moon and the removal of the physical order on this planet. Some survive this enormous event, which has to be a cosmic one. The potential of this type of event has been studied and advanced by the scientific community for the past ten years, and it has come to be the conviction that an event like the one described here is credible. They don't say this because they are bothering with the Bible; they say it because of research and study that have brought this conviction. This is what the Bible forecasts: a global event that completely shatters everything of the physical order of this world. The more that we look at the times and what has happened of recent dates, the evidence is that we are continually approaching the Day.

It can sound doomsdayish, but I didn't invent the language. Not only did the Bible say it, but it is being said by those who study the skies today and look at the facts of earth's history and what has happened before and what is inevitable. The director of NASA and AIMS, David Morrison, said that we will have no notice. That is the nice thing about the Hollywood scenarios. Everybody gets a crack at it first, and there is some opportunity for a preemptive strike. But the director said, "The first notice you will have is when you feel the ground shake beneath your feet and then you see the explosion of light coming over the horizon toward you."

"Pastor Jack, why do you talk about this?" you may ask. Because the Bible prophesies that we live in times that are approaching the climax of history. The Bible shows that there is a gathering of the Church unto Himself, that Jesus is coming for His people. How does that relate to the Rapture?

Paul unfolded it for us in his letter to the Thessalonians: "For the Lord Himself will descend from heaven with a shout, with the voice of an archangel, and with the trumpet of God. And the dead in Christ will rise first. Then we who are alive and remain shall be caught up together" (1 Thess. 4:16–17). "Caught up," in this verse, is the word *harpazo*. We shall be raptured together.

Then we who are alive and remain shall be caught up together with them in the clouds to meet the Lord in the air. And thus we shall always be with the Lord. Therefore comfort one another with these words. But concerning the times and the seasons, brethren, you have no need that I should write to you. For you yourselves know perfectly that the day of the Lord so comes as a thief in the night. For when they say, "Peace and safety!" then sudden destruction comes upon them, as labor pains upon a pregnant woman. And they shall not escape. But you, brethren, are not in darkness, so that this Day should overtake you as a thief. You are all sons of light and sons of the day. We are not of the night nor of darkness. Therefore let us not sleep, as others do, but let us watch and be sober. For those who sleep, sleep at night, and those who get drunk are drunk at night. But let those of us who are of the day be sober, putting on the breastplate of faith and love, and as a helmet the hope of salvation. For God did not appoint us to wrath, but to obtain salvation through our Lord Jesus Christ, who died for us, that whether we wake or sleep, we should live together with Him. Therefore comfort each other and edify one another, just as you also are doing. (1 Thess. 4:17–5:11)

God has not appointed us to wrath, the Scripture says. What is the time of the Rapture? We read in Revelation 6:17, "For the great day of His wrath has come, and who is able to stand?" On the day of the E Quake—the last shattering event, which breaks everything of this world—there will be wailing of lamentation of those who remain alive on the planet because that great city (not a specific place on the planet but the great city of humanity, the great structures of our politics and our economics) will be destroyed in one hour.

INEVITABLE TRIBULATION

This that is prophesied in the Scripture is called the visitation of wrath, "the great day of His wrath has come." We just read that God has not appointed His own to wrath. But Jesus said, "In the world you will have tribulation" (John 16:33). Jesus' use of the word *tribulation* makes clear that He was referring to the struggles and trials that go on through all of history and increase in their difficulty.

Someone gave me a copy of Thomas Kinkade's magnificent work, *Simpler Times*. It is a beautiful book of some of his paintings accompanied by words that recall when life was more sedate, more casual, and more wonderful as we think of things in a more rustic order. It is nice to think back to things like that, but we live in a highly intense world. There are some beautiful things about our world as it is; I don't feel bad about everything just because it is intense, but life has become stress filled.

In this arena as things continue to increase, there are times that are very beleaguering and wearying. The number of earthquakes globally continues to increase; a factual study has confirmed that. Horrendous disasters continue; for example, a hurricane in Central America wreaked such havoc that thousands upon thousands of people had to be buried quickly to forestall an outbreak of disease caused by exposed bodies. Many, many things in our world shake and break.

But the Lord Jesus said, "After those days there will come the sign of the Son of Man in heaven." (See Matt. 24:29–31.) There will be the sound of a trumpet. He described it this way: the sun is dark and the moon is dark; islands are moved out of their places; the stars fall from heaven. Obviously, an incredible meteor shower takes place.

The whole world has an appointment with wrath, just as Jesus has an appointment when He will come and take His own away to be with Him. The timing of the Rapture is simultaneous with the impact of the E Quake. You may ask, "What will people think when folks are suddenly gone?" I'll tell you what they will think. They won't even notice it. "How could that be if millions of people are suddenly taken away?" So great will be the cataclysmic disaster sweeping over this world that people will assume that anybody who is missing went in the tidal wave, died in the tremendous fires that followed, or was swallowed up by the great fissures in the ground when whole communities disappeared. People will just be gone in the midst of it all.

People sometimes think that when the Rapture takes place, many people will suddenly say, "I was wrong. They were right." They won't. They will curse God in heaven, blaspheme Him, and say that the great day of His wrath has come. They will ask to be hidden, but they won't call out in repentance. The Bible says that people have set the course of their hearts now. There will not be a sudden transformation of these people because they suddenly experience an awakening.

ROBES WASHED IN THE BLOOD OF THE LAMB

This scenario is tremendously sobering. It brings us to see the significance of the exchange between John and the elder. The elder asks, "Do you know who these are?" and John says, "You know, these are the ones that have come out of the great tribulation and have washed their robes in the blood of the Lamb."

You recall that upon their arrival, there is great rejoicing. Revelation 7:9–10 portrays them with palm branches in their hands, which symbolize what will probably take place. Palm branches in the culture of that day indicated that a great triumph was being celebrated. Following a victory in warfare when the conqueror was leading the troops into the city, people waved the palm branches. I've got to tell you, it reminds me of that good old song: "When the Saints Go Marching In": "Lord, I want to be in that number when the saints go marching in." Amen! A great, great day is coming.

The reality of that day will come about, and notwithstanding whatever may be mocked or whatever may be anticipated positively, that day is ahead, and we will move in with great triumph.

Let's have a rehearsal right now. Read verse 10 with me: "Salvation belongs to our God who sits on the throne, and to the Lamb!" Hallelujah! This will be the triumph song of the saints.

I mentioned earlier that the word *saint* in the Bible refers to anybody who puts his faith in the Lord. The robes were washed white in the blood of the Lamb. Cleanness before God is not achieved by any work of mine or yours. It is done through the power of the Cross. You come to Jesus, He calls you to Himself, and He calls you to live as His own.

The figure the Bible uses of the Church is the figure of a committed bride. She is engaged to become a bride, and she lives as faithfully now as she will then. It is unfortunate that we live in a society of cavalier, casual attitudes toward sexuality, which are indifferent toward anything of purity either before or after marriage. The Scripture describes the joy of real commitment of people in their personal relationships, and it describes us in our walk with Jesus. He has washed us to make us His own, and He calls us to walk as His own until the day we are gathered into His presence as His own. Do you want to be that kind of person? Say, "Amen!"

ULTIMATE DELIVERANCE AWAITS

The Rapture texts we have been examining tell us a combination of things. The first is the promise of being caught up together; it is available only to people who have washed their robes in the blood of the Lamb. Hear me, please. If you have never received Jesus Christ as your Savior, you are a sinner who needs a Savior. I have received the Savior, but I do not consider myself your superior for having done so. The sobering question is, Do you have a Savior?

My friend Don Moomaw, the former pastor at Bel Air Presbyterian Church, was Ronald Reagan's pastor before and during his time in the presidency. When he went in to see the president as he lay near death following an assassination attempt, Don's first words were, "Ronnie, do you know things are right?" The president nodded. "How do you know?" Don asked. President Reagan said, "Because, Pastor, I have a Savior." I have a Savior. If you don't have a Savior, the first and most significant issue for you is to settle that. Come to Jesus.

The second thing is the practical truth of the ultimate deliverance that awaits us all. I was seventeen years old, and it was two days before Christmas when the brakes on my tragically dilapidated car went out as I approached an intersection. The accident was my fault. The car that I hit spun around in a semicircle and went about a hundred yards down the street. The driver of the other car, I soon discovered, was a pregnant woman. I absolutely panicked: first because of the accident, and second, because I was concerned that either she or the child had been injured. It is a long story and a blessed one in the long run, but it took six months before everything was settled. The baby was fine, she was fine, everything was fine, and God greatly shielded us through that.

The police had come, and I was sitting in my car waiting while they were filling out some papers. My dad had arrived from home and was talking to the police and verifying that everything was covered in terms of the family's responsibility. I was sitting there, and with all my heart I said, "Oh, Jesus, I wish You would come right now." Have you ever done that?

Well, He didn't, but He took me through. He didn't take me out, but He took me through. The Lord will always take you through. One day, though, He will come and take us out. We don't know the day. I think it is important for this value to be reinstated in many believers who have been affected by the world's cynicism and have adopted the axiom, "This is slower than the Second Coming." The Bible says, "Do not be deceived, God is not mocked" (Gal. 6:7). He is coming. He is coming.

We need to gain this perspective: just as Paul was seized when his life was in jeopardy, the Savior is going to capture us away as this cataclysmic disaster strikes the world. We will be caught away in a seizure of ecstasy into the presence of the Lord.

With those things before us, let this reality sink into your soul: whatever you are enduring right now the Lord is going to take you through, or maybe, in just moments, He will take you out.

I remember learning this song as a child:

Oft-times the day seems long, our trials hard to bear,
We're tempted to complain, to murmur and despair.
But Christ will soon appear to catch His Bride away,
All tears forever banished in God's eternal day.

Then the chorus of this touching lyric by Esther Kerr Rusthoi says,

It will be worth it all when we see Jesus,
Life's trials will seem so small when we see Christ;
One glimpse of His dear face all sorrow will erase.
So bravely run the race 'til we see Christ.

If you have trusted Jesus, keep running the race, especially at the struggle points where you get weary. And remember, Jesus is coming. He is going to come, and if He doesn't take us out, He is going to take us through.

If you have never received Him, He is reaching your way today. Receive Him.

9

THE CONFLICT
OF THE AGES

REVELATION 12

In this chapter, I want to talk about the conflict of the ages. We are dealing with this book on the convergence of a battle that began before our world existed, and it will climax, if not in our lifetimes, in the time of the existence of this planet. That climax is what the book of Revelation is about, but it reports on the agelong struggle.

We can look at the conflict of the ages in different ways. We can look at it as it bears on the duration. There is a time, a symbolic figure we will see, of 1,260 days. This figure of speech is used elsewhere in the book of Revelation and represents a period of time sometimes called "a time and times and half a time" (or three and one-half years) and in other references, 1,260 days. The time of the struggle covers the period of the crucifixion, resurrection, and ascension of Christ along with the outpouring of the Holy Spirit—all the things that happened in just a few weeks two thousand years ago—until the present and even until Jesus Christ returns.

There is another way in which the struggle bears on each of us. It has to do with personal struggles, the things you and I go through in our lives.

I want to examine the cosmic struggle and the agelong struggle of the church age against the works of darkness, then the personal issues for you. The picture is wrapped up in the symbols of three persons: a woman, a Child, and a dragon.

> Now a great sign appeared in heaven: a woman clothed with the sun, with the moon under her feet, and on her head a garland of twelve stars. Then being with child, she cried out in labor and in pain to give birth. And another sign appeared in heaven: behold, a great, fiery red dragon having seven heads and ten horns, and seven diadems on his heads. (Rev. 12:1–3)

This is one of the places where we are shown a force that has several representations in the book of Revelation. We have been studying how we see things from different perspectives. This figure, which represents different dimensions of power, or evil, is repeated in different ways, yet in much the same terminology in Revelation 13 as well as in the Old Testament prophecy of Daniel.

> His tail drew a third of the stars of heaven and threw them to the earth. And the dragon stood before the woman who was ready to give birth, to devour her Child as soon as it was born. She bore a male Child who was to rule all nations with a rod

of iron. And her Child was caught up to God and His throne. Then the woman fled into the wilderness, where she has a place prepared by God, that they should feed her there one thousand two hundred and sixty days. And war broke out in heaven: Michael and his angels fought with the dragon; and the dragon and his angels fought, but they did not prevail, nor was a place found for them in heaven any longer. So the great dragon was cast out, that serpent of old, called the Devil and Satan, who deceives the whole world; he was cast to the earth, and his angels were cast out with him. Then I heard a loud voice saying in heaven, "Now salvation, and strength, and the kingdom of our God, and the power of His Christ have come, for the accuser of our brethren, who accused them before our God day and night, has been cast down. And they overcame him by the blood of the Lamb and by the word of their testimony, and they did not love their lives to the death. Therefore rejoice, O heavens, and you who dwell in them! Woe to the inhabitants of the earth and the sea! For the devil has come down to you, having great wrath, because he knows that he has a short time." (Rev. 12:4–12)

We dealt in past chapters with explosively climactic events, for example, the tremendous earthquake that will bring about the end of our world as we know it. We discussed it in the light of Scripture and in the light of contemporary scientific opinion. We are dealing with something that is as real as the air we breathe.

We dealt with something tremendously climactic and joyous—the rapture of the Church. Simultaneous with the climactic event that brings the earthquake will come the catching away of the people of God into His presence, for God has not appointed us to the wrathful destruction of that time. What we call the rapture of the Church is the immediate capturing away to the presence of the Lord forever, and we anticipate that coming. Come quickly, Lord Jesus.

A DRAMATIC STRUGGLE

Although we are not now dealing with something as climactic, it is dramatic. It is the dramatic struggle between good and evil, God and Satan, the living Jesus in His people and the forces of darkness. It is the struggle that endeavors to damn human souls; it is the struggle that seeks to deceive human minds; and it succeeds in doing both. We come because there is a deliverance that is available from both the damnation and the deception.

Revelation 12 presents a summarizing scenario. Everything that is sandwiched between chapters 11 and 15—as well as the whole book of Revelation and the whole of history, including cosmic history—could be said to be focused on the conflict of the ages. The struggle that takes place is epitomized in three characters.

THE WOMAN

The first character is the woman: "a woman clothed with the sun, with the moon under her feet, and on her head a garland of twelve stars" (Rev. 12:1). Anyone who knows the imagery in the Old Testament knows that this is a classic way to briefly symbolize national Israel, or the Jewish people.

National Israel can refer to a small piece of real estate in the Middle East or the Jews in general. Way before there was a small piece of land, a country and nation in the Middle East, there were the Jewish people, who were called Israel because of the name of their father, Jacob. Abraham, Isaac, and Jacob—he was the third in the succession of those who became the avenue by which there was birthed a people chosen to be God's delivery system for the message of His life, truth, and love and for the gift of His Messiah to mankind. Israel is the delivery system that God arranged. He chose Israel. He said very clearly, "I didn't choose you because you were the greatest of people. I chose you because I decided I would work with you, and you would become the people." This has come at a tremendous price to Jews because this has made them the focus of Satan's animosity throughout the ages. Satan also has great animosity for everyone who names the name of the Messiah, Jesus, in his life.

The dragon's animosity is toward anything that represents God's giving of His life, His love, and His law through His Messiah, His Son, Jesus. The woman here depicts Israel, and the imagery is consistent with terminology used in the Old Testament describing Israel in the terms of Jacob, his twelve sons, and the ones who became the avenue by which biologically there came into existence the Jewish people.

THE CHILD

Second in the cast is the Child, who is the Messiah: "She bore a male Child who was to rule all nations with a rod of iron. And her Child was caught up to God and His throne" (12:5). The *she* is the Jews, the national entity through which there came the promise of Messiah and the delivery of Messiah to the world. (Of course, Mary was the instrument through which it was expressed.) As Jesus came, there was an immediate effort by the adversary, who recognized what was happening; the supernatural reality of the presence of the Son of God did not take a lot of brilliance to recognize after His ministry began. But even from the inception, there was resistance, a hope for miscarriage, the lack of room for Him to be born. Herod the king was so determined to slay the Child that he ordered the brutal killing of many children in Bethlehem. The dragon sought to kill the Child. However, He survived, Christ's ministry took place, He died and rose from the dead, and then He was caught up into the presence of the Father.

The Bible says that this is the One who would rule the nations. That exact terminology with reference to Jesus also occurs in Revelation 2:27: "He shall rule them with a rod of iron; they shall be dashed to pieces like the potter's vessels." The verse is talking about the day that Christ will come again and rule the nations. That is a quotation from Psalm 2. The book of Psalms contains a prophecy regarding a universal hatred for God's ways and Messiah so that the nations boast themselves against God, but He shall come and He shall rule with a rod of iron, as the Scripture says.

You can decide whether you will experience the rule of His love or the rule of His rod. I recommend taking the love! There is the promise of opening to His love. God's Son, the Savior-Deliverer, is the second character of the cast.

THE DRAGON

The third character is the dragon: "And another sign appeared in heaven: behold, a great, fiery red dragon having seven heads and ten horns, and seven diadems on his heads" (12:3). As I mentioned earlier, the terminology also appears in chapter 13. This terminology describes the system; it is another one of the perspectives. The term for the Beast is a different term from that for the dragon and is different in the way it describes the system. The dragon describes the *source* of all evil, Satan himself. The source, the system, manifests itself in our world in different ways as also government is exercised—government that is not always, by any means, politically formed government. There are forces that work behind the scenes. More of our world is governed by things that are never seen or voted on or raised to a place of a throne of power than any of us can imagine, though we hear of it. A darkness manifests itself throughout the world, and it has destructive power on all persons, whether or not they are directly touched by it or aware of it. Just as surely as there are stray bullets in a gang war and an innocent life is taken, so there are bullets that are striking every human being in the war that is going on for humanity. Evil has an impact on everyone in one way or another. The system is destructive.

We are told two things about the dragon. First, we are given his specific identity: "So the great dragon was cast out, that serpent of old . . ." (12:9). It identifies him with the snake that came into the Garden and occasioned the fall of man: ". . . called the Devil and Satan, who deceives the whole world." Revelation 13:14 notes, "He deceives those who dwell on the earth," referring to the Beast. It is the work of darkness.

Jesus spoke of the most drastic thing to happen to people throughout this era of the postresurrection of the Savior. It will be the deception of human minds. The worst thing in the world is not disease; it is not death; it is to be deceived about who God is. The worst thing in the world is to be deceived about truth. The worst thing in the world is to be deceived about your own identity. In the name of philosophical brilliance, casual indifference, or personal indulgence, people often say, "I'm just going to do what I am going to do!" And the sadness is the deception that dominates their minds. The Bible says that this deception will bring destruction. But *you* will know the truth that banishes deception, and the truth can make you free. Have you ever been liberated by the truth of the goodness of Jesus? Praise the Lord! Truth has a name; its name is Jesus.

We are told another thing about the dragon that is prehuman history: "War broke out in heaven" (12:7). Why are we introduced to this fact here—something that reaches far back into the distant past? We are dealing in this passage with a summary statement about evil across the ages; we are caught right now in the web of a present struggle, and no one can escape it. There will be a determination on our part of how we will fare in the struggle, and it tells us from where the answer comes.

As a matter of fact, this whole book has to do with bringing us to focus on the reality as it bears on us. But it goes back: "War broke out in heaven: Michael and his angels fought . . ." (12:7). Most people in our society know Michael only as a character in an old song, "Michael, Row the Boat Ashore." The Bible never mentions Michael rowing a boat. Michael don't row no boat, but he has a powerful sword.

In Scripture, Michael is the angelic being who appears to be the warrior leader, the commanding general of the hosts of heaven's angels. The Bible never gives him that title exactly, but his role is apparent.

The Bible describes some of this rebellion in Isaiah 14 and Ezekiel 28. A mighty being in heaven named Lucifer chose to rebel against God. When it says that "his tail drew a third of the stars of heaven" (Rev. 12:4), the term *stars* in that usage describes angelic or messenger beings. Apparently, a third of heaven's hosts were deceived by Lucifer.

By the way, sometimes people say they are in touch with an angel. A beautiful series, *Touched by an Angel,* is on TV now. The series is consistent with truth, and that is not accidental. The producers insist on it. The point is that some angels come as angels of light. Satan does. You would be very wise to check out the body of information concerning angels today. Compare what those angels say and do or what is said about them with what the Bible reveals. There are angels of deception as surely as there are angels of divine gifting and ministry who bring something of God's tenderness and message to people as the angels on the hillside did to the shepherds, "Today, to you, a Savior is born in Bethlehem."

ALMIGHTY GOD

This conflict took place; there was a casting out of those beings. The good news is that heaven was cleansed. The bad news is that they were cast down to where you and I live. That was not a divine accident. God intends for us to learn to answer for ourselves what is really the answer to one of the most common philosophical and sometimes critical questions that people will arrogate to themselves. It is amazing to me how someone taking a sophomore class in college anthropology— with a little bit of the background on human religion around the world and the pronouncements of one professor—can draw conclusions that have come to control his spiritual destiny and will damn his eternal soul. And it usually has to do with conclusions drawn on the basis of these questions: If God is almighty, then how could anything like this ever happen? If God is almighty, why does evil exist? If God is all-loving, how could such things go on? He can't be both almighty and all-loving. That argument will be made by marvelously intelligent people who, because they refuse to accept the revelation of God, categorically limit their ability to understand the answers to reasonable questions.

Let me cast the question this way: If God is almighty, how could rebellion even begin or possibly succeed in heaven, much less here on earth? People may respond, "Well, the answer is that God really doesn't have the stuff or He doesn't care." He not only has the stuff, but He also deeply cares.

We must look at the nature of God and probe it to some degree of depth, although none of us can probe it to its deepest depths. He is too vast and grand for us, and we will spend eternity coming to learn more and more about the depths of the goodness and the greatness of God. But if we consider God's nature in terms of His love and God's nature in terms of His mercy, we can answer the following questions.

GOD'S LOVE

How could rebellion or sin or the things that bring hate in the world—evil—even begin? God, the almighty Creator, is infinitely love. And for there to be infinite and complete love, it must surrender the potential of free choice and free will to any subject. Infinite love leaves free choice to every creature. The living God who made us loves so greatly, He will in no way commandeer the mind or the conscience of any of us. He will offer Himself to us in His love, then risk our rejection and also risk what is said about Him for not having done something quickly about evil.

GOD'S MERCY

How can it continue? This has to do with the part of God's nature that we call His mercy. Mercy allows God to restrain from exercising His infinite power against evil until the maximum opportunity for redemption and recovery is offered to the rebel. Rather than retaliate when you or I have done something, the One who carries the biggest stick in the universe is the One who walks the most softly because of His mercy. And puny minds that refuse to bother investigating the grandeur of the nature of God, in which there is infinite love and infinite mercy, draw their pathetically shallow conclusions by asking, "How could He even let evil begin or let it continue to succeed?"

GOD'S JUDGMENT

There is another trait of God's nature: He is infinitely just. Although He extends long mercy, swift judgment will finally come.

The dragon and the struggle bring that focus. The Bible says that there was a casting down of the dragon, and the whole enterprise of the dragon now is to attack mankind. Our struggle is the continuing conflict. The dragon ceaselessly wars, and we know that the first target is that of deceiving mankind. I have already elaborated this and the way it succeeds.

SATAN'S HATRED MANIFESTED

Another facet of the struggle is pivotal to understanding our own place and role in things as they are. The simultaneous struggle is ceaseless war with the woman (the Jews) and with the saints (the followers of Jesus). The Bible refers to all of us who have been born again as saints. We are not perfectly achieving people, but we have come under the mantle of the full forgiveness of Christ, thus God regards us as holy in His sight.

Satan hates humanity in general, but he hates Jews in particular. They were the delivery system by which the Messiah came, as the seed of the woman to crush the serpent's head and to break the back of the powers of darkness. Three-fourths of the Bible came through Jewish agency. As a matter of fact, all but one book in the New Testament was written by a person of ethnic Jewish background. So the Lord used the Jewish people to give us the Messiah and to give us the Word. The covenants were passed on, and the promises of God were passed on. Satan hates the Jewish people, whether they worship God or not.

In any pocket of our planet you will find people who hate different ethnic groups. But there is a global anti-Semitism. Why do we find people everywhere who hate Jews, just because they are Jews? And why are people taught not to like Jews?

There is only one logical explanation because it is a totally illogical proposition. Tremendous benefits have come to mankind, spiritually, scientifically, educationally, culturally, and economically, through a trail of achievement by the Jewish peoples. The Jews have been scattered around the world—the *Diaspora* is the word for it—and it is one of God's ways of blessing humanity. The only logical explanation for anti-Semitism is that something is woven into the fabric of the world mind by the Deceiver, the Archenemy, the Dragon himself who, in his hatred, has spawned that animosity across the face of the earth. Anti-Semitism is a supernatural horror.

The most horrible manifestation happened in the twentieth century in the Holocaust. It was the ultimate effort of Satan seeking to achieve the extermination of the Jews. You can read about the Third Reich, the Nazi regime, Hitler and his motivation, and those who worked with him to extinguish the Jews. The Nazi hatred transcended ordinary human animosity. A supernatural drive was behind it.

In addition to the Nazi hatred that cost the lives of six million Jews, consider the worldwide passivity of nations that knew what was taking place at that time but did nothing. The evil supernature of the dragon's enterprise was behind their unresponsiveness.

I urge people to see *Schindler's List*. Many films on the Holocaust have merit. But that film was magnificently and effectively done and told a story directly from history. What is portrayed in *Schindler's List* shows something that is so heinous and horrible that it had to be spawned in something other than unassisted, unaided, unenergized human minds. This energy comes from the works of the powers of darkness. I think people need to see something like that for two reasons. First, it is a good warning against the human capacity to let hate fill hearts and do destructive things, and we need to never forget what took place. Second, it is evidence of something so supernatural in its evil that we become all the more convinced that anti-Semitism is more than a human hatred; it is of a hellish hatred.

A RELENTLESS WAR

Let's look now at verse 17: "And the dragon was enraged with the woman, and he went to make war with the rest of her offspring." We know who the first of her offspring was, the Child, the Messiah, but He was caught up to the throne. Through the Child, a host of offspring were born again, and multiplied hundreds of millions of us are alive right now on this planet. Shout hallelujah for that because it is true! "The rest of her offspring, who keep the commandments of God and have the testimony of Jesus Christ." Because we have the testimony of Jesus Christ, Satan hates Christians too. And this relentless war goes on against us.

The book of Revelation was given to a man who was in prison because of his testimony for Christ. And it was given to show him the big picture. Jesus told him, "Take this now and tell the rest of the people." The people were going to go through the same thing John was going through, and they needed to remember the big picture in the midst of the immediate part of the picture they were experiencing. Jesus was saying, "I want you to remember that whatever your trial, you are going to come through. Whatever your struggle, there will eventually be deliverance. Whatever your pain, there will eventually be relief. Whatever your death, there will eventually be eternal life. I want you to see the big picture." That is the reason people will say, "I know what happens in the end. We win! Hallelujah!" That is what the book of Revelation was given for.

The centerpiece of it all is wrapped up in one verse in chapter 12: "And they overcame him by the blood of the Lamb and by the word of their testimony, and they did not love their lives to the death" (v. 11). Now read about the other side: "Then he opened his mouth in blasphemy against God, to blaspheme His name, His tabernacle, and those who dwell in heaven. It was granted to him to make war with the saints and to overcome them" (13:6–7).

Wait just a minute. They overcame him; he overcame them. Which is it? The answer is, "Yes." "Yes, what, Pastor?" you may ask. Yes, both things happen. There are casualties in battle. There are many who in the midst of the struggle appear to have been overcome, but their being overcome is only temporal and temporary. That was why Jesus said, "Don't fear him who is able to take the body only." There is no reason to pay reverence to the powers of this world when they can only take your life.

Was there any disdain for life in the words of Jesus? Was He unrealistic about life, its promises and its joys? Of course not. But He said that there are greater ultimate issues. Jesus would not have said, "I have come that you might have life and life more abundantly," if He took this life casually or indifferently. He wouldn't have healed the sick, He wouldn't have fed the multitudes, He wouldn't have shown the great glory of God's forgiveness and grace, He wouldn't have broken demon power to set people free to live, and He wouldn't have blessed children if He didn't care about this life. But there is a greater issue than this life, and one of the problems of our humanity is the shortsightedness in this regard. We are particularly vulnerable to it in North America where we have far more comfortable lives and, as believers, far less persecution than people in most parts of the world.

THE PERSECUTED CHURCH AROUND THE WORLD

We cannot forget the persecuted church around the world. Not long ago a *Los Angeles Times* headline read, "Christians Under Fire in India." The story began, "The rape of four nuns was only the latest in a raft of attacks on churches and missionaries. Many observers blame the rise of Hindu nationalism, some say officials have participated in the violence." The long article detailed what was happening in India. Around the world every year tens of thousands of believers in Jesus Christ are put to death for one reason—they are followers of Christ.

North America at this particular time, especially the United States, is governed by a notion that goes something like this: the Christian culture was the dominant culture for too long; to balance things with the past, we won't defer to Christians anymore. That is one of the reasons I want to commend the editorial team of the *Times* that decided to carry the article about persecuted Christians in India. Mainstream newspapers rarely acknowledge that Christians suffer around the world. Praying for the persecuted church should be an ongoing practice.

We can do other things. The Christian Rescue Committee provides a way of escape for people who are persecuted for their faith. Within three days of the founding of the Christian Rescue Committee, the committee learned that fifteen Christians in Saudi Arabia were put in prison for having conducted a home Bible study. Money was provided for an emissary who, with papers from Washington and the authority of the State Department, went to the Saudi government to say, "Here, we are asking for this to take place." And with the U.S. government backing, not funding, the Saudis let them go, and the fifteen people were released from prison and they were brought back. That is just one success story.

Someone may logically ask, "It is prophesied that Christians are going to suffer and they will go to heaven, so are we getting in the way if we rescue people?" Let me ask, do you plan to go to heaven? Yes, of course! Would you like to walk out of your church on Sunday, be shot, and go right after the service? Probably not. We have missions to serve, lives to live. We have people to reach with the love of God. There is reason for us to take action without seeming to be whimpering, whining, or arguing against the possibility of persecution.

THE DRAGON AND YOU

How does the big picture apply to you? The dragon is after you personally. That is not a joke. His tactics are varied, and they wear you down by wearying you. Look with me at lessons we can learn about this principle of trial through triumph.

The first lesson is that there are no quick victories in a long war. Have you ever prayed for something to happen when you faced a difficulty, and *bang!* within minutes, hours, days, or even a couple of weeks you got an answer and a victory? Praise God! Did you ever wonder whether another battle was going to end? Do you have one right now? You may never see the end of some battles in this life. "Well, Pastor, I don't like to think that way," you may say. I don't like to think that way, either, and I am not discouraging faith. I am talking about realities.

The second lesson is that there are frequent foretastes of the ultimate outcome. Even though there is a long battle, we get frequent tastes of the ultimate victory. Good things happen. The message in Revelation is that in the middle of your present struggle, don't give up because more tastes of victory are coming, and you have had tastes already. Don't lose the taste in your mouth of victories you have received because you never know when there might be a sudden turnaround. That is not teasing with hope; that is the truth about hope.

The third lesson is that there are no cheap price tags on triumph. The struggle says, "They overcame by the blood of the Lamb." Every victory is gained through what Jesus paid for us. We also overcome through the word of our witness, our testimony. We keep going forward to see people brought to Jesus.

Some time ago, a pastor was brought out of a country where there was severe persecution. He had been incarcerated many times for serving his congregation. He had a serious disease with a discouraging prognosis, but physicians healed him. He was out from under the oppressive system, yet he said, "I'm going back because my flock needs me, and that is where I belong." Some people are not looking for an exit for the sake of themselves. They know what their lives are about: to witness, to give, to serve, to live for the Lord.

Dear one, you may not see your present situation as clearly as the Lord wants you to see it, but it is a part of becoming evidence for Jesus in the midst of a tough situation. There are no cheap price tags on triumph. That is why we call for people to give to missions—it costs to extend the gospel.

The fourth lesson is that there are present certainties to focus our peace. Whatever you are going through, knowing this will focus your peace: "He who is in you is greater than he who is in the world" (1 John 4:4). In Revelation 2, it was said to the church at Smyrna that they would go through suffering, persecution, and trouble for ten days. The phrase "ten days" implies an indeterminate length of time. The Lord said they would go through persecution, and it wouldn't go away. But He promised, "To those who suffer death through it, I am the One who has the keys of death and of hell. You won't suffer from the second death. You will have eternal glories with Me."

Loved one, has heaven lost any of its attraction? Have you become so tied to the mundane world that the promise of heaven beyond everything you go through has lost its joy? Andre Crouch wrote a beautiful song that said it would be enough to have the Lord in this life. And the inverse is true: if you never have any of the blessings now, you need to focus your peace on the things that last—the sense of forgiveness of sins and the hope of eternity.

10 THE E QUAKE: ENDING THE BEGINNING

I looked when He opened the sixth seal, and behold, there was a great earthquake; and the sun became black as sackcloth of hair, and the moon became like blood. And the stars of heaven fell to the earth, as a fig tree drops its late figs when it is shaken by a mighty wind. Then the sky receded as a scroll when it is rolled up, and every mountain and island was moved out of its place. And the kings of the earth, the great men, the rich men, the commanders, the mighty men, every slave and every free man, hid themselves in the caves and in the rocks of the mountains, and said to the mountains and the rocks, "Fall on us and hide us from the face of Him who sits on the throne and from the wrath of the Lamb! For the great day of His wrath has come, and who is able to stand?" (Rev. 6:12–17)

Then the seventh angel poured out his bowl into the air, and a loud voice came out of the temple of heaven, from the throne, saying, "It is done!" And there were noises and thunderings and lightnings; and there was a great earthquake, such a mighty and great earthquake as had not occurred since men were on the earth. Now the great city was divided into three parts, and the cities of the nations fell. And great Babylon was remembered before God, to give her the cup of the wine of the fierceness of His wrath. Then every island fled away, and the mountains were not found. And great hail from heaven fell upon men, each hailstone about the weight of a talent. Men blasphemed God because of the plague of the hail, since that plague was exceedingly great. (Rev. 16:17–21)

On March 23, 1993, a husband and a wife decided to take pictures from an observatory of the night sky. The man had been a geologist but moved more and more into the field of astronomy. Carolyn and Gene Shoemaker at first doubted that they would get anything of any substance because of the cloudiness of the sky, but they went ahead anyway.

At one break point in the clouds, there opened a very clear picture that, as it began to distill, they saw as a comet. It was the first identification of what came to be named the Shoemaker-Levy 9 Comet.

Everyone who reads this will recognize this comet, though you may not have a particular point of reference for it. In July 1994, all of us saw the coverage in newspapers and the constant reports on evening news broadcasts of the striking of the planet Jupiter by twenty-one segments of that comet. As the Shoemaker-Levy 9

Comet broke up, its tail struck the planet Jupiter's surface, and it made waves, not just on the surface of Jupiter, but throughout the entire scientific community. The impact of an asteroid, or a comet, with a planet—something that scientists said would not happen once in a lifetime, would probably not happen once in a millennium—had been seen. From that point, newspapers carried the headline: "Asteroids: A Threat to Earth Is a Joke No Longer."

This event suddenly brought the Revelation of Scripture into immediate proximity of a reality, not simply the wild imagination of an apocalyptic prophet or poet. It is another case in point where the Bible, often deemed irrelevant by our culture, is jerked into a reality where everyone says, "Maybe this really could happen. Maybe this is real."

AN EARTHWIDE IMPACT

In this chapter, I am asking you to draw two parallel points of study with me—parallel points between Revelation 6 and Revelation 16.

Chapters 17–18 show us what occurs on this planet after the disasters about which we have just read. The disasters in chapter 6 and chapter 16 are the same events seen from two different perspectives—an earthwide impact that creates a seismic reaction that no earthquake system could occasion. It is more than merely seismic; it is a cosmic event. It is the impact of something on the order of which I just described and something we will discuss further. It is becoming more and more apparent as research broadens and deepens. Members of the secular scientific community say—with no reference to the Bible whatsoever, for this is not their study book and they are not trying to verify its contents—are dealing with the question of *when* this will occur. In this portion of Scripture, we are looking at it in the light of what the Bible says about the consummation of things on our planet.

In the book of Revelation, we see these final dealings of God: the breaking open and image of the seven seals. We discussed earlier that in Roman times, the seven-sealed book was known to be a will, sealed by seven witnesses. As the seals are broken, the will is disclosed. In the book of Revelation, we see not the will of God to judge humanity, but the will of God to deal consummately and conclusively with the affairs of this planet, to bring things to a head and a finish. They cannot be brought to a head and a finish without the visitation of appropriate, just judgment upon those who resist and have no responsiveness or will to hear the heart of the Creator or feel His desire to reach to them in love, inviting them into a relationship with Him, which will bring redemption.

The subject of this passage of Scripture is the most climactic of these seals. There are many other features of this whole outpouring of judgment in chapters 6 and 16, but chapters 17 and 18 report of the aftermath: "Alas, alas, that great city . . . For in one hour she is made desolate" (18:19). The great city is not New York City, Mexico City, Tokyo, Calcutta, Johannesburg, Cairo, London, or Paris. It is the great city of human structures that are characterized by destructive things. People invest themselves in ongoing, physiological disobedience to God—mostly in actions of sexual rebellion against the divine order. Ruin also comes through political corruption, which finally spins itself completely upon humanity, and then economic collapse occurs because the systems of humanity come to an end.

Chapters 17–18 describe the great harlot and the whole system of immorality pervading the culture. It is not a matter of simply saying, "Don't people do nasty things?" It is a matter of realizing that there has been a violation of God's moral order, and it destroys humanity. Evidence abounds around us; I don't need to elaborate or give statistics. There is sufficient evidence of superficial wounds on the face of humanity in the present economic struggles and the present political struggles that lend credibility to the proposition that they will come to a consummate conclusion. This all heads up in an event the Bible describes in terms of this massive earthquake.

THE E QUAKE

This massive earthquake converges from two passages of the book of Revelation. I would like to ask you to follow me as I go back and forth between chapters 6 and 16, so that we can see that the same event is described.

The two passages are the key to unlocking the whole of the image to help us understand the book of Revelation. They move us from the linear approach—the approach so often made to Revelation—to enabling our seeing the *prophetic* vision that it really is. These earthquakes are seen from a viewpoint distinctive to the portion of the prophetic whole of the book that is presented.

A MASSIVE CATACLYSM

First, we'll reread 16:20 and 6:14: "Then every island fled away, and the mountains were not found" (16:20); and "Then the sky receded as a scroll when it is rolled up, and every mountain and island was moved out of its place" (6:14). Both passages describe a global cataclysm, the likes of which has not been on this planet since the time of the Flood, which was more than a lot of water out of the sky. The Bible says that the planet had a different configuration before the deluge of the days of Noah. The Bible says, "As the days of Noah were, so also will the coming of the Son of Man be" (Matt. 24:37), so there comes this massive cataclysm.

GOD'S WRATH

The second parallel is that both identify the event as God's wrath: "Now the great city was divided . . . Great Babylon was remembered before God, to give her the cup of the wine of the fierceness of His wrath" (16:19); and "The great day of His wrath has come, and who is able to stand?" (6:17).

We need to understand something about "the wrath of God." The Bible reveals the wrath of God as an action distinct from all other ordinary judgments of God. The wrath of God is a final visitation. People sometimes say, "They were so mad, it was like the wrath of God." Nobody gets that mad. God never has been that mad, either. The only time that there was anything close was when God turned His back on His own Son because your sin and mine was on His shoulders. He was on the cross when blackness overtook the heavens because the wrath of God was being visited in judgment upon His Son. Apart from that occasion of God's dealing conclusively with the power and penalty of sin in that moment of breaking eternal fellowship with His own Son so that you and I might be joined to Him forever, we have no occasion of the wrath of God until the Bible speaks of it consummately and conclusively at the end of time.

Both passages could refer only to the same event since they refer to the fierceness of His wrath, the outpouring of the wrath of God. It is another indicator that these are one and the same event.

UNPRECEDENTED EVENTS

The third parallel is that both refer to unprecedented events in time and in scope. In 16:18, the Bible says, "There were noises and thunderings and lightnings; and . . . a great earthquake, such a mighty and great earthquake as had not occurred since men were on the earth." In other words, this cataclysm is unprecedented. Listen, however, to what it says in 6:17: "For the great day of His wrath has come, and who is able to stand?" The timing of this day—*the* great Day—is an unprecedented time and unprecedented in its scope.

Both refer to something that has no equal in time or history at any point. It is a different time, *the* Day. It is a different scope, the whole earth. It is something like never before.

FINALITY OF THE EVENTS

The fourth parallel is that they refer to the finality of these events. Read with me, "Then the seventh angel poured out his bowl into the air, and a loud voice came out of the temple of heaven, from the throne, saying, 'It is done!'" (16:17); and "I looked when He opened the sixth seal, and behold, there was a great earthquake; and the sun became black as sackcloth of hair, and the moon became like blood" (6:12).

This reference to the sun becoming, "black as sackcloth of

hair" and the moon becoming "like blood" is parallel to an episode in the gospel of Matthew where Jesus' disciples asked Him, "Show us the signs of Your coming and the end." And Jesus described the end times by saying, "The sun will be darkened, and the moon will not give its light" (Matt. 24:29).

On the day of pentecost, when Peter was answering the question, "What is happening here?" he described the scene as an intervention of God, by His Spirit, reaching to the world until there will come the end of the end of times. He quoted from chapter 2 of the book of Joel, which reads, "The sun shall be turned into darkness, and the moon into blood" (v. 31). And John included the words in this prophecy here in the book of Revelation. They all refer to the end, the last display of judgment that brings this unusual appearance to the heavens.

We are not talking about smog making an unusual sunrise, sunset, or moonrise. We are talking about a cloud of unbelievable proportions. The astronomers said that if *any one* of the twenty-one fragments of the Shoemaker-Levy 9 Comet that hit Jupiter had struck our planet, within ninety minutes our entire planet would have been shrouded in a dark cloud. It is astonishing and incredible to hear this report of the scientific community upon having studied the impact of the twenty-one strikes on the planet Jupiter. Just one hit on planet earth would have had the kind of effect that John referenced when he spoke of the end.

NO REPENTANCE

In chapter 16, we are reading within the context of the bowls of judgments, as well as the events that flow out of the sounding of the seventh trumpet. In chapter 10, the Bible says that the sounding of the seventh trumpet occurs over a period of time: "In the days of the sounding of the seventh angel" (v. 7). In other words, it covers a short season of time. There is not a trumpet call, and then everything happens in a moment. The trumpet sounds in the invisible realm of heaven, and then a process of things happens very, very rapidly. Incorporated in them is this event cited here. The Bible tells us that the seventh trumpet is the time of the end. It is the time also, as we will be reminded, of the gathering of the Church unto the Lord. When we come, then, to 6:12 and 16:17, we see that the same event is described, both of which present us with "the end."

Read one other reference, 16:21: "And great hail from heaven fell upon men, every hailstone about the weight of a talent. Men blasphemed God because of the plague of the hail, since that plague was exceedingly great." In 6:16–17 the Bible says, "And [they] said to the mountains and rocks, 'Fall on us and hide us from the face of Him who sits on the throne and from the wrath of the Lamb! For the great day of His wrath has come, and who is able to stand?'"

The common denominator of both events, recorded from two perspectives, is that no repentance was manifested. The people were like Simon the sorcerer in Acts 8. Peter declared, "You are poisoned by bitterness and bound by iniquity." Simon the sorcerer responded, "Pray to the Lord for me, that none of the things . . . may come upon me" (vv. 23–24). There was no repentance. There was no reaction of him falling on his knees and exclaiming, "Pray for me! I need to get right with God. Pray for me that I will be delivered from the residue of the bondage of my past." It was a selfish, bitter response: "Pray for me that this won't happen to me." The people said, "Let the mountains fall on us. Let us find a place to hide."

I was struck by the words of Carolyn Shoemaker, who said, "If such a thing as what we saw happen on Jupiter happened [I don't know if this woman even knows the Scriptures, these are her words from no spiritual perspective] people would say, 'Where can we go? Where can we hide? What can we do?'" Gene Shoemaker commented, "You would feel as though you were in an oven turned up to broil. The sky would be black everywhere, all over the world."

The cry of the people in Revelation holds no repentance; indeed, it blames and blasphemes God. There is the issue of the unrepentance of humanity in the face of so devastating a confrontation with our finiteness. And every time we face our finiteness, all of us who are honest with ourselves at the same time face our need. Not just our need for something beyond ourselves, but our need by reason of our own failure.

OVERLAPPING EVENTS

Let me note a few other points that will help us in our study. These events are described as the seals are broken, the trumpets are sounded, and the bowls are outpoured. The seals are in chapter 6; the trumpets are in chapter 8. In between is an interim, and then the bowls are in chapter 16. They are not separate events, but they unfold out of the same book. These events are interrelated, overlapping, and not all sequential.

Most of us remember having alphabet soup when we were

children. (The letters are bigger now than when I was a kid!) Because alphabet soup is all mixed in together, it was fun to find the letters and put them on the edge of your dish and spell something, maybe your name. The point is that all of the ingredients are there, but they are not in an orderly arrangement. The book of Revelation is like that. All of the ingredients are there in chapters 6 through 16, but they are not in an orderly arrangement. "Why would they not be in an orderly arrangement?" you may ask. There is a reason for it, and it is common to all of prophecy in the Scriptures.

They are described in this order because that is the order in which John received them. The prophets in the Bible prophesied not in a linear mode, but in a discursive mode. Linear mode is what we would prefer to see because this happens and then that happens and so on. The prophets described what they saw: "Then I saw," or what they heard: "And then the word of the Lord came to me saying . . ." Then they wrote what they saw or heard.

Ezekiel was a good example. He recorded even the days, for example, "On the third day of the tenth month." In the book of Ezekiel the dates of his visions are not in sequence. But if you put them in the order of the dates he received them, you would still have only the discursive order of prophecy—which means to go from topic to topic as you would in conversation with a friend where you are not necessarily pursuing a thought systematically through to the end.

I suppose someone could justifiably say, "Well, why does God do it that way?" I think there is a combination of reasons, but the foremost that occurs to me is that if God put things in a straight line, we would think that by reason of seeing the things in sequence, we understood everything. But even then we would not know because the Bible tells us that we will know only in part.

The seals, trumpets, and bowls are viewed from different perspectives. It is as the eye would behold a sphere. There is no way that I can look at any more than approximately 40 percent of a sphere with any degree of clarity and get a real picture of it. To see the opposite side, I must turn it, and then I can no longer see the first side. It is so obvious that it seems almost juvenile to use as an illustration.

Let me use another illustration. If I tried to see the surface of a sphere all at one time, I would have to peel it off and flatten it out. But if I did that, I would have to, by reason of the circular nature, break it in order to make it completely flat—or make it linear.

Or consider this: if you peeled an orange at the top and kept going while keeping the peel in one piece, you would have the whole peel to flatten out. But that long string, that linear presentation of the orange, doesn't really tell you anything about the real shape of the orange. It doesn't tell you anything about the taste or what is in it. Yet you have a linear orange. It is orange and it is in a line, but you don't have the picture of what an orange is like.

We are most familiar with this in our maps. The Mercator projection of the globe casts the northern and the southern regions of the planet in real distortion and disproportion because of the way that the sphere is flattened out.

My persuasion, loved one, is that this is what has been done to the book of Revelation for years. People want to turn it into a linear progression from chapter 4 through the end of the book, but it can't be done. It can't be done without creating more questions and problems, which are strained at and worked at until we end up with something that has a certain amount of satisfaction: "Well, we've got that thing lined up." The only problem is that anytime we think we have a prophecy lined up, we soon discover that we didn't have it as lined up as we thought. We end up speculating about everything that happens.

We discussed this point earlier, and I believe it is one of the weaknesses of what most commonly happens with prophetic Scripture, especially the book of Revelation and the life of the Church of Jesus Christ. I don't believe this book was given to us to figure out all the things that are happening. This book was given to us to say, "Many things are going to happen, but in the meantime I want you to understand." Jesus is saying, "I am with you, and we're going to go through it together. There will be a lot of trouble, but there will also be a lot of victories and we are going to win when it's over." That's what I think He is saying in the book of Revelation.

GOD'S SOVEREIGNTY

I want to move now to God's sovereignty and E Quake credibility. As I have already said, the secular mind-set of the scientific community has been somewhat transformed during the past few years. The role of Gene and Carolyn Shoemaker and David Levy in the discovery of the Shoemaker-Levy 9 Comet has been pivotal. The background to their discovery is interesting.

As a result of his involvement in atomic testing in the

Nevada desert in the 1950s, Gene Shoemaker came to see how one instant of impact could produce the scenes appearing in a number of places on our planet. Until then, conventional knowledge explained them as being of volcanic origin.

Meteor Crater in Arizona is one site that has been described as being of volcanic origin. Most of us have seen, if not visited, it. Oftentimes when you are flying over that area, the pilot will point out Meteor Crater. You see a tremendous pock mark in the planet, approximately one mile in diameter. But Shoemaker believed that it and other similar sites were the result of a comet or an asteroid impact. However, no one had found any substantial amount of material that would indicate a meteor large enough to create the crater. A crater will always be considerably larger than the object that strikes it.

Research eventually demonstrated to the skeptical scientific community of geologists that the impact events were collisions— events when the angle of the strike resulted in the complete disintegration of the meteor or a portion of a comet, or its ricocheting off the earth into a new orbit. Yet very few believers shared Shoemaker's position until he and the others discovered the comet. How interesting that the man holding this position would be the person to discover the comet that struck Jupiter, resulting in conclusive evidence for his theory. No one could deny it anymore.

It is said that when the strike at Meteor Crater took place, more energy was released than what would be released if all of the world's nuclear weapons were set off at once. Tremendous energy was released in that one event an indefinite time ago.

Less than a century ago, June 30, 1908, a fireball was seen

as far as England. The strike was on the banks of the Tunguska River in Siberia. Hundreds of square miles were flattened. Investigators expected to unearth a meteorite, but they were never able to find larger parts of an asteroid remnant. They found only fragments of possible evidence of a meteor or portion of a comet. They felt that nothing could be proved about the event.

Now many astronomers are searching the heavens, looking for asteroids that may have earth-intersecting orbits with the potential of colliding with our planet. Reasons for concern go beyond the strike in the Arizona desert. Deep beneath Mexico's Yucatan Peninsula, there is a 190-mile-wide crater that was made by a one-hundred-million-megaton impact estimated to have struck sixty-five million years ago.

WE ARE A UNIQUE RACE

Incidentally, I realize that some sincere Christians have been schooled in the notion that to believe the earth is so old is to require disbelief in the Genesis record. But I have given evidence elsewhere—as have many scholars—that it is not necessary to reject out of hand the study of paleontologists, geologists, and other scientists in the name of believing the Bible. The problem is not the possibility of the extended age of earth. The problem is the proposition (based on the remnants of ancient creatures) suggesting the evolution of man as opposed to the distinct creation of man by God. That is where the error lies.

The Bible shows very plainly that our era as mankind, the race of Adam on this planet, is fairly recent. Adam was not a name given when man passed into a unique state beyond the earlier anthropoid forms. We are talking about mankind as God created us and as God made us for a special time on this planet, which was reconditioned from some earlier season of upheaval that is not described to us in the Bible but is clearly hinted at.

That there was an upheaval is clear from Genesis 1:2, for we see the perfect creation reduced to one without form and void, with darkness prevailing on the face of the deep. It was into this chaos that God spoke "light"—and with the earth's reconditioning and restructuring, man was created and placed on this planet.

Yes, we are a unique race, and we are at a unique season today. We are not an advanced form of something that began as an amoeba in a primordial swamp and accidently arrived here now. But humankind is a special creation, designed for high destiny—and our Creator has told us how we came about and what we are about.

This whole matter can be elaborated at more length as earth-orbit-impacting asteroids are being discovered. Scientists and astronomers think they may have now discovered as many as 10 percent of the asteroids that are present. They are searching for more. By studying the orbit patterns, they can better determine whether one out there will eventually collide with earth. What took place in the strike creating the 190-mile-wide crater beneath the Yucatan Peninsula eventuated in the Ice Age. What we have out in the future we don't know.

Some life will prevail beyond the strike on this occasion that we read about in Revelation, according to chapters 17 and 18. The Bible says, "In one day it has all come to an end." Everything as we know it will be shattered and dismantled, but people will remain to observe events.

In His Word, God has forecast a time that such an impact will come about. We need to be mindful of the fact that our God is never One to wreak judgment or allow judgment to come in the natural order of things. There is always redemptive action. There is always something He is doing. This is not an escapist hope but a divine promise.

OUR DIVINE APPOINTMENT

We, the redeemed, are not appointed to wrath (1 Thess. 5). The Lord says we have another appointment. This event about which it is said, "The great day of His wrath has come" or they blasphemed God in the outpouring of the "fierceness of His wrath" (Rev. 6:17; 16:14), is simultaneous with the rapture of the Church as it is revealed in Revelation. Like this cataclysmic event that climaxes history as we know it, the rapture of the Church is shown from several viewpoints.

Simultaneous with that cataclysm, which is one of the events that happen in the context of the seventh trumpet, listen to these words of the apostle Paul in 1 Corinthians 15: "Behold, I tell you a mystery: We shall not all sleep, but we shall all be changed—in a moment, in the twinkling of an eye, at the *last trumpet*" (vv. 51–52, italics added). In 1 Thessalonians 4, the apostle Paul wrote, "I do not want you to be ignorant, brethren, concerning those who have fallen asleep, lest you sorrow as others who have no hope" (v. 13). He made clear in other references, for example, 2 Corinthians 5, that although they are already in the presence of the Lord, their physical bodies will be caught up with the Lord as we are all caught up together at the sound of the trumpet of God. The Bible describes the rapture of the Church occurring in conjunction with the last trumpet and the last trumpet sounding when the cataclysm takes place.

SHAKE-UPS IN LIFE

I realize that to a certain degree, you who are wrestling against those who have so argued for a linear approach to the book see this as a bit of a different system. I do not stand alone, by the way, in this perspective. It is not a matter of showing this as a transient opinion based on drawing texts together in a clever way. I believe the book of Revelation is given for practical reasons.

Why does the Lord show us this and say in its context when that happens, "I am going to capture you away at that moment"? I think He is asking, "Are you going through any kind of an earthquake in your personal life? Is anything being shaken up where you live? Are things shattering around you?" I wonder how many accumulated millions of dollars have evaporated in stock market dips or crashes over the years. Those things have a way of shaking up how you thought of your future in terms of retirement, especially if you are close to that time. That is hardly cataclysmic on a global scale, but it is cataclysmic on a personal scale.

When shake-ups come in your life, in your circumstances, when it seems that the earth falls from underneath you because you walked into the office and the boss told you that you had two weeks left on a job you thought you'd have for the next ten years, your world shakes up. When you come out of the doctor's office having received a very discouraging diagnosis of a physical condition, your world shakes up.

It is not a matter of being people of unbelief or doubt or thinking that God doesn't care; it is just that everything shakes. And if there is any message here, it is the Lord saying, "When the world starts to shake, that's when I am going to appear." And when your personal world shakes, He is going to appear in the middle of that too. He will step into any situation you face. You can be tremendously encouraged and your faith can be built up when you acknowledge that God's Word is true.

Through this book, you and I come together as people of God looking at the Word of God and saying, "Thank God for salvation. Thank God for revelation—His truth to us. Thank God for His presence and the confidence that He will walk with us, not only through the ultimate moment, should it occur in our lifetimes when that trumpet sounds, but also through present, personal, 'shaking' hours."

Today, recognize that you are appointed to a pathway set before you. You are urged to run with endurance the race set before you (Heb. 12:1). In running the race—although there are some pretty big rocks that you stumble over along the way and sometimes cause you to fall and think that you will never get to the end—remember that scene sometime ago when an Olympic runner was injured but continued the race. Though it was clear that he wouldn't have a chance of winning, his father came out, put his arm around him, and went with him the last part of the race. I want to tell you, you've got a Father who is going to see you all the way through to the finish line, no matter what you stumble over or what impacts or shakes your world. Hallelujah!

11

FOUR REALITIES, THREE DESTINIES

REVELATION 22

When we began our study in chapter 1 of Revelation, we looked at John's encounter with Jesus and began to discover how this book was never intended to be a book simply speculating about interesting things in the future. It has been given to us to show things about the future so that we may perceive practical values about how to live in the present while anticipating the future.

We also discussed Jesus and the Terminator. We looked at the things that ruin and terminate the life that Jesus wants to be present in His Church.

We looked at the call to come into the presence of God and there to see the Lamb as He takes the scroll. We saw how the book of Revelation is really an unfolding not just of the chapters of the book of Revelation, but of the scroll, a book within the book. We saw the breaking of the seals of the scroll and the unfolding of the release of God's will for all humanity.

Further, we examined the horrendous ending quake, the E Quake. We looked at the Rapture and the conflict of the ages. We learned how contemporary scientific investigation has provided evidence and believability for the way that the Bible says this world is going to be impacted and never be the same. That is not something we "got into" because it was in line with Hollywood's *Deep Impact* and *Armageddon.* The films are the products of the last seven to ten years of scientific discovery, which have changed the viewpoint about the prospect of this planet's future. Significant, of course, is the study of the Word to see how in our time the Lord is bringing global recognition that this is not a book of fantasy. This is not a surreal supposition on the part of a prophet who has gone mad. It is from the living God who is reaching with love to say, "Look. Understand that things aren't always going to be the way you think they are. You need to think beyond the present."

Now chapter 22 is our key text, but we are also going to relate to the four chapters it climaxes. I want to deal with four realities and three destinies.

"And behold, I am coming quickly, and My reward is with Me, to give to every one according to his work. I am the Alpha and the Omega, the Beginning and the End, the First and the Last." Blessed are those who do His commandments, that they may have the right to the tree of life, and may enter through the gates into the city. But outside are dogs and sorcerers and sexually immoral and murderers and idolaters, and whoever loves and practices a lie. "I, Jesus, have sent My angel to testify to you these things in the churches. I am the Root and the Offspring of David, the Bright and Morning Star." And the Spirit and the bride say, "Come!" And let him who hears say, "Come!" And let him who thirsts come. Whoever desires, let him take the water of life freely. For I testify to everyone who hears the words of the prophecy of this book: If anyone adds to these things, God will add to him the plagues that are written in this book; and if anyone takes away from the words of the book of this prophecy, God shall take away his part from the Book of Life, from the holy city, and from the things which are written in this book. He who testifies to these things says, "Surely I am coming quickly." Amen. Even so, come, Lord Jesus! The grace of our Lord Jesus Christ be with you all. Amen. (Rev. 22:12–21)

REASON FOR THANKSGIVING

I love the classic hymn from nineteenth-century England, "Come, Ye Thankful People, Come." It is a Thanksgiving hymn, yet its content speaks directly to this portion of our study:

All the world is God's own field,
Fruit unto His praise to yield;
Wheat and tares together sown,
Unto joy or sorrows grown.
First the blade, and then the ear,
Then the full corn shall appear;
Lord of harvest, grant that we
Wholesome grain and pure may be.

This hymn, written by a British pastor a century and a half ago, opens, "Come, ye thankful people, come, / Raise the song of harvest home." *Harvest Home* is the term in England for what we call Thanksgiving. It is the same celebration, and the same mood motivates it. He took the concept of rejoicing over God's blessing us with the bounty that we observe as we come together at the harvest season.

Then he turned the corner and took the figure of Matthew 13 where Jesus spoke of the global harvest of humanity and the two kinds of people: the ones that are wheat and the ones that are tares.

Here is stanza 3:

For the Lord our God shall come
And shall take His harvest home;
From His field shall in that day
All offenses purge away,
Give His angels charge at last
In the fire the tares [that's the weeds] to cast,
But the fruitful ears to store
In His garner evermore.

That is why the end of stanza 2 says, "Lord of harvest, grant that we / Welcome grain and pure may be."

As we conclude our study of the book of Revelation, I want these grand truths to be viewed with thanksgiving. In the same way, the writer of that Thanksgiving hymn took a horrendous reality—the fact that there will be some who will be weeds by reason of the response they have chosen as opposed to the grain—yet didn't lose the spirit of thanksgiving in the midst of something with a horrible ending. As we come to this text and study these four realities and three destinies, there is no way in the world to be anything but thankful. Even though there will be ones who are forever lost, we can be thankful that God didn't want them to be lost; they made the choice. And we can have gratitude for the love that has reached our way as well as gratitude for having received the love that opened the door to eternal blessing.

"And the Spirit and the bride say, 'Come!' And let him who hears say, 'Come!' And let him who thirsts come. Whoever desires, let him take the water of life freely" (Rev. 22:17). I don't know of any lovelier words in the Bible or in our language than these: the Holy Spirit of God says, "Come!" Come and drink of the water of life, and the Holy Spirit will live in those who allow Him to indwell them with the heart of God's love reaching to humanity. The bride—the ones who love Jesus, the living Church—says, "Come!"

Let us not be slow to extend, "Come!" to people, to show the love of Jesus so much in our hearts that we want them to know Him too. We can say, "I met Somebody I want you to know." The Holy Spirit says, "Come to Jesus." The bride says, "Come to Jesus." The Bible says, "Let those who hear say, 'Come!' and let them come and drink of the water of life freely." What beautiful words!

FOUR REALITIES

These words embody the central concept of these great, great realities and destinies. We could say that the whole Bible is laid over the grid of these four realities.

1. GOD

First is the reality of God. Jesus' words speak of the reality of God: "I am the Alpha and the Omega, the Beginning and the

End, the First and the Last" (22:13). This is a statement that "God is." "Alpha and Omega"—I was before all things, the beginning; I am beyond all things; I precede all and I will exceed all. It is the fundamental question that exists in the minds of millions, "Is there a God?" Here is the announcement of the resurrected Son of God: "I was; I will be; I have been; I will be forever. I Am." And the reality of God is set forth.

This is an inescapable reality, yet it is common in our culture to hear denial of God's existence or His love, notwithstanding the fact of the resurrected Savior and the reality that has occasioned billions of people to come to Jesus Christ. Lines from the classic Easter hymn, "You ask me how I know He lives, He lives within my heart," echo the reality of an encounter with the living Jesus. Thomas, Jesus' disciple, cried out, "I won't believe unless I put my fingers in the wounds in His hands and in His side." And Thomas bowed before Him after the resurrected Lord appeared to him. The skeptic, the cynic, may say He isn't, but He is. Jesus is the Son of God, the Lord God almighty in the flesh come to us. The reality of God is here.

The heart of God is a part of this ultimate reality. We read in verse 16: "I, Jesus, have sent My angel [or My messenger] to testify to you." These few words describe the constant outreach of the heart of God to mankind. Jesus says He is sending a messenger to you. God so loved the world that He sent Jesus. Jesus says to us, "Go to all the world and say, 'Come!'" If I ever lose that recognition, I have lost the beat of God's heart. The reality of God is not only that He is, but also that He loves. He is love. God is love in a culture that thinks love is God. It is important to get it turned around straight to understand that He is and He loves and He loves you.

2. THE WORD OF GOD

The Word of God is the second reality: "Blessed are those who do His commandments" (22:14). Let's start with the most fundamental aspect of the Word of God. Almost everyone has heard of the commandments of God, the Ten Commandments. Some attitudes about the Ten Commandments are fouled up. Too many people think they are out of date, a notion that is past its time, while others, even believers, think of the Ten Commandments as Old Testament stuff. They are not. Jesus said in the New Testament that He expected His people to understand them and teach them and live in them by the power of God. We don't earn salvation by honoring the commandments, but we can learn to live in a way that makes life work, which is why they were given.

God's commandments are benevolent. Each one was given to help us make life work, to help us avoid self-destructing so that relationships work, so that business works, so that society works. And to the degree that His commandments are scorned and disregarded, to that very degree things become confusing and destructive.

The commandments of the Lord are beautifully put in the words that are on the cover of a book written by a dear friend of mine. Pastor Ron Mehl has released a book with the title *The Ten(der) Commandments*. They are tenderly given from the heart of God to be a blessing to us.

Verses 18–19 show us something else about the Word of God, which lays a grid on these four unshakable realities:

For I testify to everyone who hears the words of the prophecy of this book: If anyone adds to these things, God will add to

193

him the plagues that are written in this book; and if anyone takes away from the words of the book of this prophecy, God shall take away his part from the Book of Life, from the holy city, and from the things which are written in this book.

The passage is about the conclusiveness, the absolute authority, of the book in a relativistic world. Dear one and friend, don't dabble with it by adding to or removing from this book because the Bible warns not to mess with it.

I am very, very careful about the Scriptures. I am never going to take away or add anything. The ultimate reality is that God has spoken.

3. THE JUDGMENT OF GOD

The third reality is the judgment of God. I don't know of anything more sobering: "But outside are dogs and sorcerers and sexually immoral and murderers and idolaters, and whoever loves and practices a lie" (22:15). We will look at this list later, but let's now consider this phrase, "But outside." They are outside what is in the previous sentence: "That they may have the right to the tree of life, and may enter through the gates into the city" (22:14). The city noted here takes us back to Revelation 21: "I saw a new heaven and a new earth . . . I, John, saw the holy city, New Jerusalem, coming down out of heaven" (vv. 1–2). This is talking about heaven, the eternal city.

Anybody who ends up outside the city is there because he didn't answer the invitation to "come!" People will be outside by reason of choice. Anyone who loses his eternal soul will have made a conscious choice.

The judgment of God mentioned here is reminiscent of Jesus' words that described heaven as a wedding party and those who come are provided a proper garment to wear. But if you don't come with the right garment on, then you are out. It is not a garment you pay for. It is provided, and you can't come in any other garb. You are clothed in the righteousness that alone comes through Jesus Christ. The Bible uses the phrase "the garments of righteousness." It doesn't have to do with "churchified" clothes; it has to do with a righteousness that clothes us with the grace and the mercy of God through the blood of Jesus Christ. I go, not exposed with the sins of my flesh, but robed in something Jesus has given me.

God's judgment falls on the uncovered souls who are exposed by their rejection of His protection. But nobody need be unclothed or uncovered. Let's understand this about the judgment of God. It is not random or arbitrary. It falls on those outside who remove themselves from the protection of the umbrella intended for them.

4. THE SALVATION OF GOD

The fourth ultimate reality is the salvation of God: "Let him who thirsts come. Whoever desires, let him take the water of life freely" (22:17). Freely there is given to us a drink at heaven's well of salvation.

Do you remember one of Jesus' conversations that amazed His own disciples? He was talking to a woman at a well at noontime. The very fact she was there at that time of day and the way she was most likely dressed gave away that she was a social outcast of the community because of her immoral behavior. The disciples saw

Jesus talking to her, and they were surprised on two counts. They were surprised that He would talk to a woman like that. They were also surprised that Jesus, a Jew, was talking to a woman who was a Samaritan. The ethnic barricade—the discrimination and the separation between the two groups—was argument enough, notwithstanding the woman's immoral life. Yet Jesus spoke to her with the heart of God, addressing the thirst in her soul that occasioned her drinking at an empty well. She was drinking at a well that offered no satisfaction, and Jesus said, "Come and drink. The water that I will give you will well up in you unto eternal life."

This "water of life" is a phrase used in the Bible to refer to our salvation. Other things are mentioned here, for example, the Book of Life. Reread part of verse 19: "God shall take away his part from the Book of Life." That reference takes us back to 21:27: "Those who are written in the Lamb's Book of Life." This references the Book, a heavenside book, where there is inscribed the name of each person who opens his heart to the love of God through His Son, the Savior.

I remember as a child learning this hymn,

Lord, I care not for riches,
Neither silver nor gold.
I would make sure of heaven,
I would enter the fold.
In the book of Thy kingdom,
With its pages so fair,
Tell me, Jesus, my Savior,
Is my name written there?

Is your name written there? The Bible says that each time a person repents and turns to the Lord, the angels in heaven rejoice. Then a writing takes place as the name is put in the Lamb's Book of Life.

Other books are noted in this same portion of Scripture, books that will be opened and there will be an accountability for the deeds that have been done in our lifetimes and judgment meted out accordingly. But the Book of Life is a part of the salvation message.

The Tree of Life and the Gates of Life are mentioned here as well. The Tree of Life is referencing the return to Paradise. You will recall in Scripture that mankind, in the perfect setting we call the Garden of Eden, had the offer of a life forever. "You are what you eat," we say, and mankind was given to feed on the Tree of Life. The endless life that was available to man at his creation wasn't available without feeding. If he kept feeding on that tree, life would go on. But if he violated trust and fed otherwise, then he would lose access to that Tree.

Genesis 3 shows that the gateway to the Tree of Life was closed. No one could access it any longer until there would come the provision of the One who would be the Savior; otherwise, mankind would continually live in sin. Endlessness of separation from God is no heaven; it is no life. And so, the Tree of Life offers fulfillment, and the Gates of Life present an invitation to glory.

THREE DESTINIES

Three destinies summarize the book of Revelation.

1. THE WORLD'S SITUATION

First is the description of the dead-end street of our world's situation: "The great city Babylon shall be thrown down, and shall not be found anymore" (Rev. 18:21). Hear these words speaking of our world and its ultimate destiny: "The sound of harpists, musicians, flutists, and trumpeters shall not be heard in you anymore" (Rev. 18:22). God is saying that the things that have been points of jubilation and creativity and artistry won't be anymore because there is no reason to play anymore. "No craftsman of any craft shall be found in you anymore, and the sound of a millstone shall not be heard in you anymore" (Rev. 18:22). The millstone is a picture of the commerce of the time. "And the voice of bridegroom and bride shall not be heard in you anymore" (Rev. 18:23). The celebrations will be no more, not even a bridal party.

I think one of the most ridiculous statements that people ever make is this: "Well, at least if I go to hell, I will be there with my friends, and we can party forever." I want to tell you, loved one, there isn't going to be any partying on earth, much less in hell. This sordid notion that life is just a kick is on short term. The Lord intends for us to enjoy life in its fullness. But all these things are temporary.

"Then the beast was captured . . . [who] deceived those who received the mark of the beast and those who worshiped his image" (Rev. 19:20). This reference looks at the world when finally everything that was under the control of the dominating spirit of the world comes to an end. It is epitomized, beginning in chapter 13 and going through chapters 19 and 20. We find this climaxing convergence of the ultimate destruction of everything that is of the Beast's system.

People ask, "Well, what does 666 stand for? Who is the Beast/Antichrist?" They raise all sorts of questions: "What about having a social security number? What about the big computer in Belgium? What about the bar code on groceries?" Everyone is messing around with these things and trying to figure out speculatively, "Does this have to do with the Beast's system?"

I am not here to tell you whether or not any of these things are of the Beast. Ultimately, requirements of the commercial world aren't the issue. The bottom line is this: the mark of the Beast is something so inscribed on your soul of the world's value system that you can't shake loose to be what you were made to be in the purpose of God. That kind of inscription grinds and engraves itself in you every time you concede to anything of the value system of this world rather than keep the values of eternity most in view.

God has not called us away from the reality of day-to-day life in a real world where there are certain business factors we need to navigate. As a matter of fact, I think that believers ought to be the most successful businesspeople because they honor the Lord in their approach to life and in their values. When these values intrude upon the world's system, they will prosper ultimately because they are the values given by God to make life work.

How often and how easily we will concede while gradually our souls are engraved upon and the Beast's system takes over. In conjunction with the fall of great Babylon, John wrote, "Alas, alas." In today's language we would say, "Ooohhh! It has all come to nothing!" That will be the final statement concerning the destiny of this world.

2. THE ETERNAL CITY

The second ultimate destiny is the eternal city. Listen to these words: "And I heard, as it were, the voice of a great multitude, as the sound of many waters and as the sound of mighty thunderings, saying, 'Alleluia! For the Lord God Omnipotent reigns!'" (Rev. 19:6). It is a ransomed host in the presence of the Lord. "Let us be glad and rejoice and give Him glory, for the marriage of the Lamb has come, and His wife has made herself ready" (Rev. 19:7).

Now we turn to this picture,

> Now I saw a new heaven and a new earth . . . the holy city . . . coming down out of heaven . . . prepared as a bride adorned for her husband. And I heard a loud voice from heaven saying, "Behold, the tabernacle of God is with men, and He will dwell with them . . . And God will wipe away every tear from their eyes; there shall be no more death, nor sorrow, nor crying. There shall be no more pain . . . Behold, I make all things new." . . . And he showed me a pure river of water of life, clear as crystal, proceeding from the throne of God and of the Lamb . . . The leaves of the tree [of life] were for the healing of the nations. And there shall be no more curse. (Rev. 21:1–4; 22:1–3)

Hear that, loved one, this is the word of the Lord describing ultimate joy, ultimate comfort, ultimate fulfillment, ultimate community, which is relationship, ultimate purpose. Don't get the shallow notion that heaven is going to be a place where you spend the rest of eternity popping grapes in your mouth while you lounge around in a Roman toga.

"Eye has not seen, nor ear heard, nor have entered into the heart of man the things which God has prepared for those who love Him" (1 Cor. 2:9). There is no way we can conceive of the eternal purpose that God has for each of us. People have said to me, "It seems to me that reincarnation has to be true because spending eternity being the same person would be boring." Not when you discover the person that you were made to be originally and have the destiny that the Creator, who is infinitely creative, has designed for you to know. God has great ideas for your future.

In regard to the eternal city, the Bible tells us that "those who do His commandments" have the right to the Tree of Life, to enter through the gates into the city. But outside are dogs, sorcerers, sexually immoral, murderers, idolaters, and those who love and practice a lie. That list can be very deceiving if we make a shallow reading of it.

Why would the Bible refer first to dogs? Is God kind of spitting in the faces of human beings? No. This has to do with the inclination of people who reject the divine order and the truth of God's purpose in their humanity by insisting on their animal heritage and yielding to and arguing for their animal instincts. And it is part of the religion of our society.

There are two systems, both of which require faith. An honest scientist who rejects the revelation of God's description of how all things came into being, especially humanity, will admit to you that the system that is so enshrined in our culture of the animal origin of man is a proposition of faith too. It can't be proved. It can't be demonstrated. They can construct charts, but the concept doesn't play out honestly and scientists will show you that. It requires faith to believe, just as it requires faith for us to believe that God created the first pair, breathed into them the breath of life, and there was special creation. Each one of us is the product of special creation, not of a process of evolution. It takes faith to believe either system.

Our society must finally devise a system of belief in its animal origin if it is going to concede to yielding to its animal value system. It is not just a matter of dog eat dog in the workplace. It is not just the rule of tooth and claw on the field or battle. But it is the things that are conceded to that eventually become destructive. Sexual values, approaches, and expressions are reduced to a basic yielding to animal instinct. You are never going to hear me talk against the relative joys of sexual fulfillment and the possibilities and the grandeur and beauty that God has given to us as human beings. But He has given a very specific design— these things are to be applied and exercised and rejoiced in within the marital relationship. The Bible also says that the marriage bed is to be kept pure.

I warn you to listen to the Holy Spirit and not the latest movie about practices in our culture today. Animal instincts drive too much in our culture.

Then sorcerers are mentioned. The Greek word that is translated "sorcerers" is the word from which we derive our word for "pharmacy," *pharmakeo*. *Pharmakoi* is the form here, referring to the toxicity of what we call substance abuse. (This is the refined term we use for ingesting or partaking of things that we know full well will alter our state of consciousness or provide some means of escape from our responsibility or real humanity.) These toxic things are joined to a participation in the demonic— the two are linked.

Let me say very bluntly and directly that exposure to most of the things related to what we call substance abuse is oftentimes equivalent to exposure to demonic control. I didn't say that using medicine is exposing yourself to the demonic. I am talking about the abusive use of things that are commonly known in the culture to alter what we are supposed to be. When I say I don't want to be a human and I take things that make me something other than that—whether it is for escape, indulgence, or whatever it may be—I open myself to superhuman demonic power that produces the subhuman. "Sorcerers" refers to this kind of participation and people's submission to demonic control through voluntary use of harmful substances.

Next are the sexually immoral. Isolated instances of sexual disobedience are serious matters. Even a one-night stand has severe implications. But the subject here is far more severe than that. The sexually immoral have a habitual commitment to breaking the bonds of what is the divine order for the human personality. They have the casual attitude of gratifying themselves at the expense of shattering somebody else's humanity. I am sorry to say that I have met a few people who name the name of Christ and live that way, thinking it has no implications. I want to tell you with passion—not with fury, but with a fearful passion for your soul—that if you think that way and you name the name of Jesus, there is no covering for what you do. You are "outside." The Scriptures say so not because you had a moment of weakness and fell, but because you have repeatedly chosen to exhibit a casual attitude toward God's order and ways.

The bondage is deep, and the destiny is horrible. I weep. I implore anyone in this category, "Come! Come and drink of the water of life." The woman at the well who had indulged in what was a behavior pattern was empty, but Jesus offered her the living water. Live in the richness of God's love, and the artificial will no longer be tantalizing.

Murderers are next in the list. We could easily dispense with that word and say, "Not very many of those." But according to the Scriptures, this has to do with more than the taking of a life by gunpoint or knife. Some people are ruled by anger and hate. In Jesus' own words He made equivalent the pattern of hatred and fury toward people with murdering. It shouldn't be hard to figure out why. With a set of words you can cut somebody off at the knees and hinder his ability to make progress in his life just as surely as if you stabbed him in the back and his life was cut short.

Idolaters—I could write a whole book on them. They substitute the superficial for the eternal, enshrine the carnal over the spiritual. It is not that they are tripped up by their humanity and flesh sometimes; it is that they choose to enshrine it and bow before the great god of selfish indulgence.

The last group includes "whoever loves and practices a lie." I was at a store the other day, and someone asked the clerk for directions to a certain street. The clerk stopped for a moment and said, "Turn left and it is the third signal down there." Another clerk said, "No, it's the fourth signal." And the first clerk thought and said, "That's right." Then he turned back to the person and said, "Sorry, it's the fourth signal. I lied." What he meant was, "I made a mistake." But I hear that kind of terminology used all the time. I have watched this phenomenon rise in our society in the last ten to fifteen years. This is enormously significant that a common mistake is considered a lie.

There is coming a trivializing of lying. Those who love and

practice a lie are different from people who are motivated to untruthfulness by a moment of fear because they become panicked and are afraid to admit what really happened. I am not pleading the righteousness of that behavior, but I am saying that is not loving and practicing a lie.

Loving and practicing a lie have to do with a lifestyle of rejecting truth consciously. Loving and practicing a lie have to do with the practice of deceiving other people intentionally. The tongue can't be trusted because the heart has become habitually committed to untruthfulness. It is a part of the world system as well. I suppose the worst expression of loving and practicing a lie is choosing to discount revealed truth in order to deify one's contrary position to God's truth.

In academia this is very common to love and practice a lie, to be unwilling to come and face the truth. One of the greatest academics of this century, C. S. Lewis, described his pilgrimage from his atheism to faith, not because he was a man who was desperate for something of religion, but because he was a man who wanted to know truth. The more honest he became with truth, the more he came to recognize that his whole system didn't hold water. He finally submitted to God's truth. I would challenge any person who has been told in the name of some intellectualized approach to life that there is little practical reality in the things of God to look a little deeper. You have been sold a very shallow bill of goods, no matter how intellectualized it may sound or in what impressive terminology it may be cast.

3. THE LAKE OF FIRE

I conclude these observations by pointing to *the third destiny: the lake of fire.*

Look with me at Revelation 20:11–15: "Then I saw a great white throne and Him who sat on it, from whose face the earth and the heaven fled away." There is the ultimate accountability. There is no way to escape standing before God. "I saw the dead, small and great, standing before God, and books were opened. And another book was opened, which is the Book of Life. And the dead were judged according to their works, by the things which were written in the books." Notice *books* is plural. "The sea gave up the dead who were in it, and Death and Hades delivered up the dead who were in them. And they were judged, each one according to his works. Then Death and Hades were cast into the lake of fire. This is the second death. And anyone not found written in the Book of Life was cast into the lake of fire."

It is not considered fashionable, by any means, for a preacher to bother to read this. This is called "hell, fire, and brimstone" faith and tradition. Usually, it is accompanied by pulpit beating, pounding, and storming, and some say that went out sometime in the nineteenth century or early in the twentieth century for truly thinking people. To the contrary, I believe that thinking people should take very seriously the most wonderful man in human history—His name was Jesus of Nazareth. He said that He was the Son of God, and He lived like it. He said that He was going to die for the sins of the world, and He did. Then He said that to prove He was who He said He was, He would rise from the dead, and He did. He is alive forevermore, and the book of Revelation is the book where He says, "This is how it all pans out in the end."

The last part of the destiny is this horrible option. The One who talks to us about the horrible option is the same One who died to make a way of release from it and rose from the dead to enforce the viability of our eternal life if we will come to Him. And He is the One who says, "The Spirit says, 'Come!'" He is the One who says to you and me who know Jesus, "Are you saying, 'Come'? Are you reaching out to people?"

To what degree do these ultimate destinies govern your relationships and your reach? Come. Come.

I had been in the ministry for thirty years and written hundreds of songs and preached thousands of sermons. One Sunday afternoon I was driving down to the church, and I was thinking about people who had received the Lord that day and how happy I was about that. Then John 3:16 came to mind: "For God so loved the world that He gave His only begotten Son, that whoever believes in Him should not perish but have everlasting life." I realized it's all there. God is. God so loved the world that He gave His Son. The Son came to speak the love of God to us. God spoke—and speaks. And then Jesus died that whoever believes in Him should have eternal life and should not perish. There are the judgment and the salvation.

I thought of all the songs I'd written, I had never written a song about John 3:16. There are other songs surrounding John 3:16, and there didn't need to be another one. Yet I thought, *This is a gift of mine and I would like to write a song about it.* And it wasn't really a conscious prayer.

Now, this has never happened to me at any other time, but *bam!* right there, this song just came to me. It was so simple and so singable. Here it is:

God so loved, He so loved the world
That He gave us His only Son
That if we would believe in Him
We may have everlasting life.

The following verse in the Bible says: "For God did not send His Son into the world to condemn the world, but that the world through Him might be saved."

God so loved, He so loved the world
That He gave us His only Son
That if we would believe in Him
We may have everlasting life.